D0918363

THE MEANING OF CZECH HISTORY

BY *Tomáš G. Masaryk*

Portrait of Tomáš G. Masaryk by Max Švabinský, 1902, from Jan Herben, T. G. Masaryk (Prague: Sfinx Bohumil Janda, 1946).

THE MEANING OF CZECH HISTORY
BY *Tomáš G. Masaryk*

*Edited and with an Introduction
by René Wellek
Translated by Peter Kussi*

*The University of North Carolina Press
Chapel Hill*

The University of North Carolina Press
wishes to express its gratitude to the Friendship
Fund and to the Masaryk Publications Trust
for assistance in the publication of this volume.

Library of Congress Cataloging in Publication Data

Masaryk, Tomáš Garrigue, Pres. Czechoslovak Republic,
    1850–1937.
    The Meaning of Czech history.

    1. Czechoslovak Republic—History—Addresses,
essays, lectures. I. Wellek, René, ed. II. Title.
DB205.M33 1974   943.7   73–16126
ISBN 0–8078–1227–7

12-20-78

Contents

Introduction

    The meaning of Czech history? Can there be an express meaning, sense, or idea, we may ask skeptically, not only of Czech history but of all history? Modern analytical philosophy has taught us to distrust all words, however hallowed by tradition. We have to define the meaning of "meaning" more closely. Some would say that the meaning of a nation's history is only another way of speaking of its leading theme, its dominant character, or its specific contribution to the history of civilization. We can hardly doubt, for instance, that Greek democracy or Roman law constitute achievements attributable to only one nation. A value judgment is implied: we consider Greek democracy and Roman law to be more important in the subsequent course of history and even to us today than, say, Greek religion or Roman technology. But the word "meaning" can mean also something more. It can mean "mission"; it can be a call to action, a program, a political or moral demand. Thus the Hebrew prophet saw the meaning of the history of Israel in a special relation to God, and a Christian sees the meaning of all history in the salvation of mankind through Jesus Christ. Abraham Lincoln spoke of his nation as "dedicated to the proposition that all men are created equal" and others later spoke of "manifest destiny" or simply of the "American dream."

    Masaryk uses "meaning" in this later, wider sense. His concept of Czech history is a program, a demand, a call to action, an appeal to his nation, which he wanted to become free in terms other than those claimed by nineteenth-century nationalist ideology. Masaryk aimed at giving an ethics, a national ethics, to his people, one that would at the same time be universal, yet anchored in the peculiar history of the nation.

The writings here translated, in which he first formulated his ideas, date back to the 1890s, except for one item, a speech on John Hus given 1910. To understand them properly, something should be known of Masaryk's career and the background of his ideas.

Born in a small town (Hodonín) in southern Moravia in 1850, the son of a coachman on an imperial estate, Masaryk succeeded in gaining an education in the primary and secondary schools in Moravia and Vienna and then at the University of Vienna, where he took a doctor's degree in philosophy in 1876. His dissertation discussed "The Nature of the Soul According to Plato." After a year of study in Leipzig—where he met Charlotte Garrigue of Brooklyn, New York, whom he married after a hurried trip to New York in 1878—Masaryk submitted, as required, a second thesis to the University of Vienna, "Suicide as a Social Mass Phenomenon." It allowed him, in 1878, to become a *Privatdozent*, i.e., he thereby acquired the right to lecture at the university, though with no compensation other than the paltry fees paid by the students enrolled in his course. But only a *Privatdozent* could be called to a regular salaried professor's chair. When in 1881 the university of Prague was divided into a Czech university and a German university, the Czech university was looking for young talent. Masaryk was made *Professor Extraordinarius* of philosophy in 1882. He went to Prague, he tells us, without knowing a soul there, unacquainted with his colleagues, unfamiliar with the cultural situation in Bohemia.

But this outsider changed things very quickly. *Suicide as a Social Mass Phenomenon* appeared in German in 1881. In 1883 he founded a weekly, *Athenaeum*, expressly devoted to scholarship and criticism of scholarship. At the university and in students' societies, Masaryk lectured on "David Hume and the Calculus of Probability" and "Blaise Pascal," topics unheard of in Bohemia, where philosophy remained in the orbit of German thought. In 1884 he published two little books in Czech: *The Theory of History Ac-*

cording to the Principles of Thomas Henry Buckle and *On the Study of Works of Poetry*. In 1885 a book in Czech appeared called *The Foundations of Concrete Logic*, which is more clearly described in the subtitle of the later German edition (1887) as the "classification and organization of the sciences." Masaryk was on the way to becoming a major force in the university and in the expanding life of Czech scholarship, but soon the pursuit of the academic life was over for him.

In 1886 he was plunged into the controversy over the forged manuscripts supposedly written in the thirteenth and even the ninth centuries, "discovered" by V. V. Hanka in 1817 and 1818. In spite of the rejection of their genuineness by the founder of Slavic philology, Josef Dobrovský, and the several later attempts to expose their fraudulence, the manuscripts had been defended by the great historian of Bohemia, František Palacký, and even by the author of the first scholarly book on Slavic antiquities, Pavel Josef Šafařík. The manuscripts maintained their authority largely unimpaired until Masaryk opened the pages of his review, *Athenaeum*, to his colleague Jan Gebauer, then the most competent student of Old Czech, who accumulated completely destructive evidence against the authenticity of the two manuscripts ("Králové dvůr" and "Zelená hora" in Czech, "Königinhof" and "Grünberg" in German), based mainly on their use of incorrect grammatical forms and word formations. Masaryk supported him with arguments drawn from an insight into the impossibility of the social conditions depicted in the poems and by aesthetic arguments: the poems, he concluded, were romantic fabrications evoking a nonexistent dim past of the Czechs which were totally at variance with historical evidence.

We might think today that this was an obscure philological quarrel of no more importance than the authenticity of Chatterton's Rowley poems or of the Shakespeare "documents" forged by William Henry Ireland late in the eighteenth century. But this is not true of the Czech manuscripts: they threw the history of the ancient Czechs and the entire history of the Slavs into confusion. Only after the manuscripts had been exposed as forgeries was it possible to gain a correct image, not only of old Czech history and literature, but also of the conditions of all Slavic nations in the early Middle Ages. But Masaryk did not think of this controversy as a simple matter of scholarship: it was for him primarily a moral question. It meant a decision between falsehood and truth, national illusion and sober self-knowledge. It is today difficult to imagine the hysteria that this whole campaign evoked: Masaryk and his associates were attacked in the press as national traitors, as robbers of palladia, as "hyenas gnawing at the bones of the greatest patriots."

Thus Masaryk became a controversial public figure and soon a politician; he was elected in 1891 to the Austrian Parliament as a member of the Young Czech party. But he resigned his seat after two years, finding himself more and more in disagreement with the policies of the party. He returned to the university and to free-lance journalism. *Athenaeum* had perished, but in 1893 was replaced by a monthly, *Naše Doba* (*Our Time*), of which he was the editor-in-chief. There he began to publish his reflections on Czech history and politics, as the years of his activity in the Austrian Parliament made him strongly feel the need to formulate his program and to study the past of his nation to support his program. Eventually four books resulted from his reflections: *Česká otázka* (*The Czech Question*, 1895), largely devoted to a sketch of the history of the Czech revival in the early nineteenth century; *Naše nynější krise* (*Our Present Crisis*, 1895), concerned with what was then the current political situation; *Jan Hus* (1896), a little treatise on the Great Reformer and martyr who was burned at the stake in Constance in 1415; and *Karel Havlíček* (1896), an elaborate study of the life and teachings of a prominent journalist and politician who played a great role in the 1848 revolution and the reaction following it. To these books one must add "Palacký's Idea of the Czech Nation," a long article first published in 1898 in *Naše Doba* and then as a pamphlet in German in 1899.

Our selections contain the bulk of *The Czech Question*, an almost complete translation of the article on Palacký's "Idea of the Czech Nation," a speech on "Jan Hus and the Czech Reformation" delivered in 1910 which seemed to summarize his views more effectively than the earlier book, and a brief extract from the book on Havlíček. The selections are, on occasion, slightly abridged by dropping allusions to contemporary events that would require elaborate explanation. Masaryk was adept at expressing himself in a number of genres, and his expository prose has a characteristic style that can be described as a cross of two linguistic milieus—conversational speech and rhetorical language. In the present anthology, however, it would have been difficult to do full justice to Masaryk's style without sacrificing clarity and preciseness. Many of the selections represented here were regarded by Masaryk himself as drafts or "chips from a workbench" rather than polished essays. While the translator suggested something of Masaryk's literary personality, his main object was to strive for fluency in English, and to eschew an interlinear, narrowly literal version. On occasion, he allowed himself a certain freedom of modernization and rephrasing. The biographical index should make identification of little-known names easy.

If these books amount to a political program, they certainly go about it in an unusual way. We are, in *The Czech Question*, plunged first into a discussion of the Czech revival at the end of the eighteenth and the beginning of the nineteenth century. Masaryk starts with what he must consider the desolate state of the Czech nation in the eighteenth century. The counterreformation after the battle on the White Mountain (1620) had deprived the nation of its upper classes; only some of the Catholic clergy preserved a national consciousness while the peasant masses survived or rather vegetated in passive torpor. The reforms of Emperor Joseph II (1780–90) brought welcome toleration to the surviving remnants of underground Protestantism, but they also increased centralization and with it the imposition of a unitary language, German. The reforms also loosened the peasants' feudal ties to the soil and, in effect, turned the tide against German dominance by allowing an influx of peasants who knew nothing but Czech into the Germanized cities. The spread of the Enlightenment ideas from Germany and, ultimately, from France, the distant effect of the French Revolution (however suppressed) freed the new Czech intellectuals from the confines of Austrian Catholicism. Masaryk discusses Josef Dobrovský (1753–1829) in some detail, for he was the founder of Slavic philology and the compiler of both the first scientific Czech grammar and the first scholarly history of Czech literature (both published in German). Masaryk shows that Dobrovský, though a Catholic priest, took considerable pride in the Czech Hussite past and that his fears of the possibility of the extinction of the language were not inspired by defeatist skepticism but, as Masaryk nicely phrases it, by "the love of a mother for a weak child." The very fact that Dobrovský was a freemason shows that he had emancipated himself from the counterreformation spirit. Masaryk is severe on Josef Jungmann (1773–1847), the compiler of the first many-volumed dictionary of the Czech language and the translator of Milton's *Paradise Lost*, Gothe's *Hermann und Dorothea*, and Chateaubriand's *Atala*, a man generally considered to be one of the foremost "awakeners." Masaryk chides him for his liberal Voltairianism, his irreligion, and cynicism and considers him to be the fountainhead of modern Czech "liberalism," which meant to him antireligious indifferentism. Jan Kollár (1793–1852), the Slovak who wrote a lengthy poem, *The Daughter of Sláva*, and a pamphlet, "On the Mutuality of the Slavic Nations" (1837), appeals to Masaryk much more. He was the first Protestant in the galaxy of "awakeners," a Slovak (though writing in Czech) who posed the question of the Slovaks, then under the heel of the Magyars. Masaryk, partly of Slovak descent, had many Slovak contacts and sympathized greatly with their plight. Kollár was the propounder of a cultural Pan-Slavism. Masaryk grants Kollár's romantic affinities: his illusions about the ancient peace-loving Slavs derived from the idyllic picture painted by Herder, the violence of his nationalism and hatred for the Germans, and the fancifulness of his dreams of an all-Slavic language. But he treats Kollár with great sympathy, defending even the contrast Kollár drew between the rapacious Teutons and the meek Slavs against a Russian scholar, Ivan Sobiestansky (1856–1896), who had tried to demolish the pastoral image of the ancient Slavs. Kollár, Masaryk argues, was a true humanist; he believed in the brotherhood of man and was filled with the ideals of his Protestant forebears.

But the men who spoke most intimately to Masaryk were František Palacký (1779–1876) and Karel Havlíček (1821–56). Palacký was the greatest Czech historian of the century; his *History of Bohemia* (1836–75) exalted the Hussite period and the teachings of the Bohemian Brethren as the culmination of Czech history and made all Czechs again conscious of their glorious past: Protestant, humanist, democratic. Masaryk can fully endorse, in the nineties, Palacký's famous letter to the Frankfurt Diet, in 1848, in which he rejected the invitation, protesting that he was no German and defended the Austrian Empire as a bulwark against despotic Russia, hoping, however, that Austria would be transformed into a federation of free nations. Palacký's "Austro-Slavism" was in many points still acceptable to Masaryk in 1898. Like Palacký he distrusted Czarist Russia and considered Czech hopes in Russia a deception; like Palacký he wanted a federalized Austria that would be organized by nationalities. He did not believe in state rights, in the restoration of the Bohemian crown, as he knew the power of the Germans in Bohemia and Moravia and was also loath to surrender the Slovaks to the tender mercy of the Magyars. They, like the Czechs who yearned for a restoration of the old Kingdom of Bohemia, could and did assert the historical rights of the Hungarian crown. Masaryk thus had to deplore some of the later developments of Palacký's policies. Palacký identified more and more with the Bohemian nobility and gave up the natural rights claims in favor of the appeal to historical rights. It was a comprehensible shift if we consider the settlement between Austria and Hungary of 1867 and the enormous rise of Prussian power. Palacký had lost hope for a break-up of historical Hungary and clung to the historical rights of Bohemia against the increasing pressure of pan-Germanic nationalism.

Masaryk rather turned from the later Palacký to Karel Havlíček, a journalist who had relentlessly and courageously battled for the rights of his nation, arguing forcefully on two fronts: against the reactionary Austrian government and against the revolutionary radicalism of some Czechs in 1848. Havlíček had paid for his boldness with a long internment (1851–55) in southern Tyrol and had come back home only to die soon, a broken man. Masaryk shares Havlíček's rejection of "historicism": the uncritical and indiscriminate idealization of the past. He shares his suspicion of Russian intentions and can subscribe to Havlíček's slogan "A Czech, not a Slav," which Havlíček had propounded after his years (1843–44) in Russia, where he had acquired a first-hand knowledge of Russian Slavophilism and the Russian Orthodox church. The journalist's "realism" makes Masaryk gloss over Havlíček's Catholicism and lack of interest in the Protestant past, though in his book on Havlíček, Masaryk made a special effort to show him as a deeply religious man. Besides, Havlíček appealed to Masaryk because he posed the social question; he knew that the Czech revival could not be complete without enlisting the sympathy and cooperation of the working classes and ending their exploitation.

Here is then the gallery of heroes or demiheroes: Dobrovský, Kollár, Palacký, Havlíček, and more doubtfully Jungmann. In passing, Masaryk pays his respects to the memory of the first great Romantic poet, Karel Hynek Mácha (1810–36), though he could not approve of his Byronic pessimism, and to the Hegelian philosopher Augustin Smetana (1814–51). He speaks also of the role of natural science. Jan Evangelista Purkyně (1787–1869), a physiologist who was famous in his time, is called upon to support Masaryk's hope for an increase of the scientific spirit and scientific interests among the Czechs. He felt their dependence on the Germans in the field of science to be a sign of Czech backwardness, for the whole thrust of Masaryk's arguments was always directed toward one goal: to raise the Czechs morally and intellectually so that they would become truly worthy of being free.

The Czech revival is seen then by Masaryk as a rebirth, not only of the language and of national consciousness—as this would make it parallel to the contemporary revivals in Greece, Bulgaria, Serbia, Croatia, Romania, Hungary, Latvia, Lithuania, Estonia, and Finland—but also a rebirth of what to him is the specific glory of Czech history: its Protestantism, which Masaryk interprets not in the theological or polemical terms of the Hussite Reformation but as an assertion of intellectual freedom, of the right for the search for truth against any authority, and, even more importantly, as an assertion of the common humanity of man, the truly Christian practice of brotherhood, and the love of one's neighbor. Masaryk thus exalts the martyrdom of Jan Hus while ignoring—even in the booklet specifically devoted to Hus—the details of his conflict with the Council of Constance. He sees Hus rather as a direct forerunner of Luther, quoting Luther's declaration of himself as a Hussite. Hus is admired for his fortitude and moral zeal rather than for the power of his arguments against the abuses of the church of his time. Masaryk, like Palacký, exalts the Hussites who fought for their faith and defended Bohemia against the crusades sent for decades to bring them to submission. He admires their military leader Jan Žižka (1376?–1424), though he recognizes his fanaticism and deplores the violence and cruelties of the Hussite wars. His heart goes out rather to Petr Chelčický (1390?–1460?), a pupil of Hus who came to reject all violence, all war, all institutions, and even the state itself. Chelčický expounded what could be called a Christian anarchism; in his *Net of Faith* (c. 1440–43), he condemned all inequalities among men; the nobility and the clergy in particular, he argues, have been unfaithful to Christ's commandments. Tolstoy was attracted to Chelčický and wrote an introduction to a Russian abridgement of the *Net of Faith* in 1896, at a time when his own convictions had been reached.

Chelčický is the spiritual father of the Unity of the Bohemian Brethren. Masaryk does not discuss their teachings in any detail and pays no attention to the considerable changes in their doctrines as they have been analyzed, for instance, in Peter Brock's excellent study of *The Political and Social Doctrines of the Unity of Czech Brethren* (The Hague, 1957). The Brethren are simply Masaryk's ideal of a Christian community, the model for Czech life. Masaryk occasionally deplores the fact that after the German Reformation they aligned themselves more and more with Lutheranism, which had become dogmatic and even served the political aims of German princes. The catastrophe of the battle on the White Mountain, when the Czech estates (which had elected a Calvinist, Frederick of the Palatinate, king of Bohemia) were defeated by the imperial forces, was in Masaryk's view inevitable. The Czechs had declined morally and spiritually. Masaryk makes much of the year 1487, when the feudal dependencies of the peasants on their lords were tightened; in his eyes this was the sin that brought about the division of the nation into sharply defined classes. The peasants, who had been reduced to the status of serfs, had become apathetic and indifferent to national aspirations. Thus the battle of the White Mountain, and its aftermath, was the consequence also of internal moral decay, just as the revival of the nineteenth century was the result of a moral rebirth of the nation, to its reaching back into the glorious, good, Christian past.

During the time of "darkness," one figure stands out: Jan Amos Komenský, better known by his Latinized name, Comenius (1592–1670), the last bishop of the Bohemian Brethren. He went into exile in 1627 and wandered through Poland, Hungary, and Germany before he found a last refuge in Holland. Comenius was famous in his time as a pedagogical reformer (which earned him

an invitation to England in 1641) and has been recently redis-
covered as an encyclopedic philosopher. Masaryk added him to
his gallery of Czech heroes (though I am not aware of any detailed
comments), not only because of his sufferings, but also because his
ideal of education ("things" rather than "words," the graphic
rather than the verbal in education) was to him a further element
in his program for the rebirth of his nation. The Czech future, as
he envisaged it, would be based on religious freedom, democracy,
and national independence. But all this could not be achieved, in
Masaryk's view, without general education, without a complete
separation of church and state, without the moral firmness and
intellectual clarity of every single Czech, who, Masaryk felt, had
as a member of a small nation to prove himself to be not merely
equal but actually superior to his potential rivals. Masaryk's love
for his nation, his concern for his future, his exaltation of its special
mission in history, should not, however, obscure his view that
nationality is only a step to humanity, to brotherhood, to true
Christianity. Masaryk thus combatted what he considered the false
patriotism, the patriotism that indulged in rhetoric about the glorious past but had no conception of its actual nature and no desire
to live up to its ideals. The Czech of his time, he argued, preferred
to sit back in angry but passive resignation rather than put his
hands to work. Work, even petty daily work, was a persistent
theme of Masaryk's exhortations. The Czechs must make their
way by work, not only manual, of course, but also work with the
brain and with machines. Masaryk did not distrust technology and
science: he considered resistance to them a sign of backwardness.
Science means truth, a knowledge of truth, and hence a rejection
of legends and superstitions. The battle against the forged manuscripts was a part of this "demystification" of the past. It later led
him, at great personal risk, to expose the absurd superstition of
ritual murder, for which, as late as 1899, a Jewish vagrant, Leopold
Hilsner, had been condemned to death. It made Masaryk also dis-
approve of the sudden artificial glorification of the memory of
the earliest missionaries to Moravia, Constantine-Cyril and Methodius, who, Masaryk argued, had no influence on the Czech nation,
since it emerged only after the destruction of the Moravian Empire
early in the tenth century. He felt that assertions of a continuity
with the past of the Slavic church served only the purposes of

growing clericalism and that the saints were used as a counter-weight against the memory of Jan Hus.

The aim of history is the establishment and realization of the ideal of humanity. But "humanity" is an ambiguous term and Masaryk has often been grievously misunderstood. Humanism never meant to him sentimental humanitarianism, nor is a secular humanism ever set in opposition to a belief in God, as the term is frequently used in the United States. Nor does Masaryk share the view of the neo-humanism of Irving Babbitt and Paul Elmer More, which emphasizes man's opposition to nature, his duality. Rather, humanism is for Masaryk the perfection of man conceived as a religious, moral, and responsible being. Democracy is another name for this ideal. It is not simply advocacy of universal suffrage or equality before the law: Masaryk was no egalitarian democrat in the sense of the French Revolution. Democracy meant to him the belief that every man should be able to strive for perfection, that no outward constraint, no social barrier, no economic or national oppression should bar his way to the realization of his humanity. When Masaryk stresses the natural rights of man, he does so out of reverence for the immortal soul of every single man.

If we look back at Masaryk's view of Czech history, we cannot think of it as an "objective," scholarly history or even philosophy or theory of history. Masaryk scarcely makes an effort to enter into the minds of bygone people, to reconstruct their outlook in its historical setting, for he does not care for the past in itself but mainly for the consciousness and conscience of his contemporaries and their descendants. The past for Masaryk must stay alive to shape the future. Thus selection from the past of a "usable" past, the creation of a tradition that would become a force in the present and future, seems an overriding duty to Masaryk.

Masaryk saw the dilemma of the modern Czech in the conflict between his Catholic faith—or his liberal, lukewarm indifferentism—and the only pride he could take in the history of his nation. He had to appeal to the Protestant past, to the great century between the death of Jan Hus at the stake in 1415 and the ascendency of the Habsburgs in 1526, the century in which the Czechs stood alone in defiance of all Western Christendom, had a government that, if not technically a republic, did disavow the rule of the king and was later headed by a king, George of Poděbrady (1438–71), the only Czech on the Bohemian throne since the extinction of the native dynasty of the Přemyslids in 1304. The Czechs, Masaryk knew, were the only people who had to face this inner division. They could, he thought, overcome it only by renouncing their Catholicism or indifferentism and becoming men of faith again. But Masaryk knew, of course, the enormous obstacles that stood in the way of a renewal of faith and he disapproved of mere political conversions to Protestantism. He realized that this call for a new religion was that of a voice in the wilderness. In his first book, *Suicide as a Social Mass Phenomenon*, he had diagnosed the increased incidence of suicide as due to the decay of religion, to what today is called in Nietzsche's terms "the death of God." Even then he hoped for a new religion that would give the same sense of security as the old Catholicism, but he somewhat ruefully admitted that waiting for the organization of a new religion was hardly a practical prescription for the social ills of his time. He then could conclude only with a quotation from De Tocqueville's *Democracy in America*: "When the religious views of a people have once been shaken, there should be no hesitation in promoting enlightenment at any cost, because, though an enlightened and skeptical people presents a sorry sight, there is nothing more terrible than a nation at the same time ignorant, coarse, and unbelieving."

Masaryk himself had joined the Reformed church in 1880 and had even signed the Apostles' Creed, asserting the divinity of Christ. His American wife was a Unitarian. For a time he seems to have contemplated the career of a preacher and even a missionary. He took part in the celebration of the hundredth anniversary of the Toleration Patent of Emperor Joseph II at Klobouky in Moravia, in 1881, which was attended by several English clergymen. But his zeal for the church seems to have cooled rather quickly, possibly because he had plunged into a detailed study of the works of John Stuart Mill and David Hume. But they did not shake his basic religious conviction, as his late writings or his *Conversations with Karel Čapek* testify. God gives certainty and unity to his profoundly and primarily ethical view of life. Theologians have objected that Masaryk's God had no specific conceptual content and that Masaryk, in spite of his high regard for the figure of Christ and the historical role of Christianity, was no

Christian in a strict sense. Several of the main tenets of Christianity —the fall of man, the atonement of Christ—were quite foreign to his way of thinking. Still, Masaryk could say that he never, even for a moment, had been an atheist and that he considered the religious question the only important question in life. The ethical starting point of his religion is, however, obvious. The difference between right and wrong was something absolutely clear and self-evident to him, something immutable, independent, and inexplicable by utilitarian considerations. The concept of God and immortality was for him a guarantee of the eternal difference between right and wrong. The affinity with Kant is striking, though Masaryk rejected what he considered Kant's subjectivism.

Masaryk's moral authority dominated the Czech struggle for independence abroad. When he entered Prague as the first president of the newly independent country, he entered with a moral authority unparalleled among the statesmen of his time. The Czechoslovak Republic during his presidency (1918–35) became an island of democracy; social, national, and religious equality; and a great educational workshop, in spite of many shortcomings and problems, which even Masaryk's influence could not solve. It was beyond his power and that of his successor, Eduard Beneš, to prevent the destruction of his work by German conquest, which, fortunately, he did not live to see. (He died in 1937 at the age of eighty-seven.) But his spiritual legacy was very much alive, even during the cruel Nazi occupation. His son, Jan Masaryk, spoke over the radio from London to kindle the spirit of resistance throughout the long war years and came back as foreign minister of the new government after the liberation in May 1945. Again the beginnings of a new freedom were crushed by the Communist coup of February 1948. Jan Masaryk either was murdered or committed suicide, the first symbolic victim of the new tyranny. Tomáš Masaryk was, during the years of Stalinist domination, either deliberately ignored or grossly vilified as an enemy of the Russian Revolution and of communism. Street signs bearing his name were changed and monuments were melted down. But his memory could not fade. When the shackles began to loosen again, particularly in the spring of 1968, Masaryk's spirit and writings returned. His name was frequently invoked; a book published in 1967 by Milan Machovec expounded Masaryk as a great moral,

"existential" philosopher and national hero, and he reprinted gener-
ous extracts from Masaryk's writings, though the work preserved
a Marxist veneer. A reprinting of most of Masaryk's writings
was planned: Karel Čapek's charming and moving *Conversations
with T. G. Masaryk* (1937), which contains also an exposition
of his philosophical and political views, was reprinted in 1968;
and, miraculously, *The Czech Question* and the small but meaty
booklet, *Ideals of Humanity* (1901), appeared in March 1969, after
the Russian invasion, with a courageous postscript by the editors,
Josef Špičák and Josef Navrátil, who spoke of the Czech nation's
renewed struggle for its political independence. Today, after the
shameful invasion of 21 August 1968, Masaryk's writings are again
on the index: even books about him are forbidden, but the nation
—with the exception of a very small group upheld by the presence
of some eighty thousand Russian troops—is now as united as it was
under the Nazis in passive resistance, full of anger and even hatred
for the invader. The old Pan-Slavism, the century-old illusions
about Russia are dead.

Masaryk had loved Russia; he visited there in 1887, in 1888, and
in 1910 and called on Tolstoy twice. His largest work, *Russland
und Europa* (in English called *The Spirit of Russia*, originally published in German in 1911) was an elaborate intellectual history of
Russia which is still unsurpassed in its massive learning and acute-
ness of analysis. Dostoevsky, in particular, was a constant challenge,
as was Tolstoy with his total teaching of nonresistance to evil.
But Masaryk was also highly critical of Russia: before 1917, of
the oppressive Czarist regime, the Orthodox church, mystical
Slavophilism, and atheistic radicalism; after the Russian Revolution, of communism and Stalinism. The events of the last years
only confirm his diagnosis.

Masaryk's views on Czech history were, of course, challenged
in his time. Opposition came from political quarters, for instance,
from Josef Kaizl (1854–1901), his colleague in the Young Czech
party, who in 1898 became minister of finance of Austria-Hungary.
In a little book, *Czech Thoughts* (*České myšlenky*, 1896), he
argued that the Czech question was a national question and had
nothing to do with religion. The awakeners of the early nineteenth
century were liberals in the tradition of the French Enlightenment not that of the Reformation. More seriously, professional

historians queried the general conception and rejected many details of Masaryk's interpretation. The most formidable critic was Josef Pekař (1870–1937), who in 1912 elaborately attacked Masaryk's Czech philosophy (*Masarykova česká filosofie*). He argued, like Kaizl, that a gulf divides the national revival of the early nineteenth century from the Czech Reformation, that the ideal of humanity expressed by Herder and embraced by Palacký has nothing to do with the fervent Christian beliefs of either the Hussites or the Bohemian Brethren. Dobrovský was an enlightened Catholic priest who approved of the Hussites only because they spread the Czech language. Comenius is not mentioned by him. He considered the old Czechs to be "enthusiasts," *Schwärmer*, who, because of a mere opinion, went to their deaths unafraid. Also Jungmann, Šafařík, Kollár, and even Palacký were religious liberals who either did not appeal to the Protestant tradition or thought of it only in national and social terms. Pekař quotes Palacký saying: "What for the sixteenth and seventeenth centuries was the idea of church and religion, the idea of nationality is for our age." Pekař dismisses Masaryk's philosophy of history as an artificial construction without support in reality and even in conflict with it. He disputes also Masaryk's view of the year 1487. It was no landmark year, notable only for a resolution that was passed in the Bohemian Diet forbidding the sheltering of peasants fleeing from the land and their overlords. The peasants had been vassals long before. The Hussites (and even the Bohemian Brethren) accepted the feudal order and did not demand the emancipation of the serfs. Nor is it true that the outcome of the battle of the White Mountain can be ascribed to the moral decay of the nation. Its record of toleration, piety, and learning was exemplary in the sixteenth century. Pekař —who became a great authority for his immensely erudite books on St. Wenceslaus, on Žižka and his time, and on the conspiracy of Wallenstein—concluded that Masaryk had invented a national mythology.

Masaryk held fast to his view, defended it strenuously several times, even in *The Making of the State* (1925), without mentioning the name of Pekař. Palacký alone, Masaryk argues, is sufficient to prove the thesis of the religious foundations of Czech humanism. He asks whether it can be chance that three of the main "awakeners" (Kollár, Šafařík, and Palacký) were Protestants. Scholars such as J. B. Čapek, in his book on *Czech Literature in the Period of Toleration*, have succeeded in tracing a direct continuity from Protestantism to the revival, particularly in Slovakia, where the counterreformation was less stringently enforced. But whatever impartial scholars may conclude about specific issues, the charge that Masaryk overrated the continuity between the Czech Reformation and the revival is ultimately beside the point. Masaryk was not and did not pretend to be a professional historian doing research in archives. Admittedly he did not know or did not care about the exact nature of the theological disputes that brought about the death of Hus and the Hussite wars. He approved in general of most of the teachings of Petr Chelčický and the Bohemian Brethren. But what he cared about most and what he succeeded in stating eloquently is the continuity of the national ethos: a concern for truth—however differently interpreted in different times —for authenticity, as we would say today; a concern for our fellow man and his rights; a passion for justice and freedom and thus for democracy, conceived of not simply as liberal egalitarianism but as a free society with equal rights and duties, bound together by a common loyalty, not only to the nation, but to the good of humanity. One can call Masaryk's view of Czech history "myth" or "mythology," if we understand "myth" not in the depreciatory sense of lie or deceit but as an ideal by which men have lived and died. Masaryk believed passionately (though he was a sober man on the surface) in the truth of his conception as he believed in God and Providence and thought that every nation is assigned its role in a divine scheme, has its own specific place and mission, is governed by an idea or a central meaning. One can doubt these assumptions and consider all history a play of meaningless, irrational, almost animal forces, as Tolstoy argued in *War and Peace*. One can embrace a deterministic view of history, explaining everything by economic conditions, technological changes, and the class struggle, as did Marx. One can, like Carlyle, believe in the power of heroes, great men, the supermen who shape history. Or one can, as Masaryk does in principle, believe that history is moved by ideas in the minds of men. The vocabulary with its Hegelian and ultimately Platonic overtones should not conceal the very practical, concrete content of Masaryk's conception and its historical efficacy. It is enough to compare the Czechs as they were in the nineties—or at least the average man who was nationalistic, religiously indifferent, socially unaware—with the men who grew up under the republic of Masaryk. Something of the new ethos, which is Masaryk's ethos, while rooted in the past, survived all of the terrible events of the years 1938–68. "Socialism with a human face," even in its very phrasing, could not have become the slogan of the Communist intellectuals who wanted to reform the government and the party and to repudiate the ugly period of repression and persecution (such as the rigged Slánský trials) without the memory of Masaryk's humanism. Again critics can object that there is a gulf between Masaryk's religious humanism and the reform communism of the spring of 1968. Masaryk, after all, had, in his book *The Foundations of Marxism* (1899), criticized Marx from an ethical and religious point of view, even though he accepted many of his criticisms of capitalist economy and was in favor of socialism, if socialism meant social reforms, a concern for the working classes, and a serious attempt to solve their grievances. But there is also a common ground, a common ethos, a yearning for freedom, for truth, for authenticity, which confirms the basic rightness of Masaryk's idea of Czech history.

René Wellek

THE MEANING OF CZECH HISTORY
BY *Tomáš G. Masaryk*

 CHAPTER I

Jan Hus
and the Czech Reformation

So this is where Jan Hus breathed, lived, and suffered.
... In the twelfth year of the fifteenth century he must have come
here twice, three times. We can well imagine him pacing these
ramparts, gazing with longing toward Prague—the city where his
work began, the city where his work could never be completed.
He came here to Kozí Hrádek, he returned to Prague, and at last
he embarked on his fateful journey to the Council in Constance.

But this air we breathe today is not the air he breathed, this dust,
this parched soil is not the ground he walked on. This place is in
ruins, physically it no longer connects us with Hus. Besides, his
ashes were scattered over every corner of the globe.

Bodily, physically—nothing. What is it then that still binds us
to Jan Hus? At first, when I received the invitation to speak here,
I hesitated. To tell the truth, I was afraid that this may turn into
a pilgrimage, and I instinctively recalled the words of the teacher
of Jan Hus: "Let the dead bury their dead." How harsh are these

From "Master Jan Hus and the Czech Reformation," a speech delivered at
Kozí Hrádek, 17 July 1910. Published in Tomáš G. Masaryk, *Jan Hus: Naše
obrození a naše reformance* (Prague, 1923), pp. 141–59. Kozí Hrádek is a
castle in southern Bohemia, now in ruins, where Hus found a temporary
refuge after being banished from Prague in 1413.

[*3*]

words of Jesus, warning us that we should be concerned about spirit only, that only spirit can bind us to spirit.

Everything that surrounds us here is dead. And, to tell the truth, I was afraid that we too may be dead, that we periodically go through this ritual of burying the dead because we are not sufficiently alive to the spiritual world. But I am glad to say that after my experience here my doubts were laid to rest, and I think there is good reason to hope that we are proceeding in the spirit of Hus after all.

You inhabitants of the south have often made this pilgrimage to the memory of Master Jan Hus. Recently, we have been hearing more and more about your part of the country; we have been reminded that southern Bohemia was the cradle of our reformation, the birthplace not only of Jan Hus but of many other exceptional men who determined the character and direction of our reformation movement: Tomáš Štítný, the astronomer-philosopher Křišťan of Prachatice, Matěj of Janov, Žižka, the Taborites, Mikuláš of Pelhřimov, also the Adamites and other sects, and finally Petr Chelčický. All these men came from southern Bohemia, and it is thus, we are told, no accident that our religious movement originated in the south. Historians maintain that our southern countrymen tend to be contemplative, frank, honest, and sober. The southern landscape is supposedly monotonous, keeping the mind from distraction and favoring contemplation. We are also told that the social and economic circumstances in this part of the country had the same basic character in the time of Hus as they do today: great wealth of the church, large number of wealthy monasteries and estates, creating among an oppressed people a sense of injustice and a longing for equality. These circumstances were largely responsible for the democratic nature of the Taborites, the simplicity of the Taborite worship as well as the communistic and chiliastic enthusiasm of people deprived of both spiritual and material bread. No, it is certainly no accident that the Reformation originated in these parts. But we must not push this idea too far. Let us remember that eastern and northeast Bohemia also nourished the Reformation, let us remember Moravia; Milíč of Kroměříž was an important forerunner of Hus, also Stanislav of Znojmo and among the Taborites let us recall Martin Loquis—above all— Komenský, and also Blahoslav. All the Czech lands, as well as

Moravia and Slovakia, were strongly involved in the Reformation movement. Prague, too, played an important part, particularly its university. It was the university professors of Czech origin who first proclaimed the great Reformation movement and who placed themselves under the ideological influence of Wycliffe.

Austria, too, was a highly heretical land at the beginning of the fifteenth century. Perhaps the Waldensians had prepared the ground there; it is difficult to say. There is no question that social conditions played an important role, that the wealth of the aristocracy and clergy led to discontent and helped to strengthen the reform movement—but to what extent? How strong were these various influences? Bohemia was not so large at that time that the reform movement could be attributed to a particular locality or ethnic group. It is not enough to explain it by economic or any other conditions. Clearly, the response that our reformation evoked throughout Europe testifies that it was spirit—mainly the Czech spirit—that set the great struggle in motion.

Speaking of the south—I must mention that this region also produced the first Jesuits. The Czech counterreformation had its start here, and today the south is supposedly the staunchest bastion of Catholicism. The social conditions that prevailed at the time of Hus underwent little change, yet the country is calm and peaceful. These considerations help justify our approach to the Czech Reformation, for our emphasis will be on its moral and spiritual rather than on social or economic aspects.

Let us recall that Hus and his forerunners began as moral reformers. This was already true of Štítný. Nor was concern about morality limited to scholars, philosophers, and clergymen. Emperor Charles IV, who had helped the church gain inordinate wealth and power, became frightened of the results of his policies and launched corrective measures. In Prague, the predecessors of Hus delivered moralistic sermons from the pulpits. In those days, pulpits played the role of today's newspapers and books in disseminating ideas. The sermons were directed at the improvement of morality in the towns and at the reformation of the wealthy classes and rich clergy.

Hus began his career with the same kind of anticlerical sermon, directed against moral decay. "Ye are the salt of the earth," the founder of Christianity told his disciples. "But if the salt have lost its savour, wherewith shall it be salted?" That is the main thrust of Hus's sermons against clerical immorality. This relentless and genuine anticlericalism, justified by his own high moral principles and life, created bitter hostility against Hus. Soon, even those who agreed with his fundamental position abandoned him and left him to his fate.

An important source of moral striving came from moral theologians, particularly the Englishman Wycliffe. The Czech university, in fact the entire Czech country, became a seeding ground for the teaching of Wycliffe's ideas. The Taborites, in particular, consistently followed not only the teaching of Hus but the more radical precepts of the English philosopher. Hus actually had no wish to abandon the dogmas of the church, but he was excommunicated because of his anticlericalism. Above and beyond the Pope he placed the council, above and beyond the council and entire church he placed Scripture, proclaiming Christ the true head of the church. Also, he advocated that priests be stripped of their office whenever found guilty of mortal sin. The Taborites went even further in their anticlericalism. This was their hallmark —the courage to eliminate the clergy altogether. That is why they attached no importance to ritual and introduced a simple new worship readily understood by the people. The abolishment of clerical offices was connected with the doctrinal rejection of transubstantiation. The Taborites maintained that reason had led them to the conclusion that bread and wine could not contain the body and blood of Christ. This proved too much not only for Žižka but for Chelčický as well, and Chelčický strongly opposed the Taborites on the issue of transubstantiation. It certainly speaks well for the moral fortitude of the Taborites that they steadfastly rejected this cardinal point of medieval religious dogma.

The struggle of the Czech people against Rome and against all of Western Europe was glorious, magnificent. In the course of these battles the voice of Chelčický was raised against the use of the sword, then the Bohemian Brethren came into being. After Chelčický, the mild Brethren found their spokesman in Komenský, but within a relatively short time, the Hussite movement underwent inner decay. The Brethren suffered from persecution, not only by Rome but by rival Hussite factions as well. In the end the elite of the Bohemian Brethren had to leave the country, with thousands of families taking part in the exodus. At the same time, our reformation began to lose its national characteristics and merge with the German and West European Reformation.

The counterreformation ensued, and it was not until the onset of the tolerant policy of Joseph II that the small survivors of Brethren and Hussites dared to proclaim their Protestant faith. The counterreformation, which actually had its inception even before the battle of the White Mountain, triumphed in the course of the succeeding century. It was a terrible period in the history of the Czech people and in the annals of the human race. Three-quarters of our land was confiscated and squandered away to foreigners.

Toward the end of the eighteenth century, as our movement of revival gathered momentum, our nation began to emerge from the depths of degradation to which the counterreformation had consigned it. This renascence of ours is still far from complete. All of us who realize what is at stake have the high duty of helping this movement grow and prosper.

I have presented a brief sketch of the course of our reformation. Without going into historical analysis, it is evident from the tremendous richness and diversity of this phenomenon that a true "re-formation" was involved, a work of spirit and spirit alone. Of course, no spirit exists without a body, the various social and physical circumstances played their part, but as a great historical process our reformation can only be understood in terms of Czech national spirit. For this reason, it is important for us to be clearly aware of the issue involved in the Czech Reformation movement, its principal ideas and directions.

The Middle Ages had systematically constructed a monumental theocratic edifice. Theocracy literally means the rule of God. On one side, the spiritual power led by the Pope, on the other side the temporal power led by the Emperor and the feudal aristocracy. The church as the foremost spiritual power, the state as its secular ally and servant. All human endeavor was connected with the church, led by the church and dedicated to it. Hus and the other Czech reformers—and ultimately the entire Czech people—challenged this enormous temporal and spiritual might. Actually, our reformation only demanded that the church practice what it preached; it demanded a return to the apostolic era. If Christ was the founder of Christianity, then his disciples—the clergy—must live on the model set by the apostles. Apostolic morality meant love, effective love, as well as candor and simplicity. The book containing Christ's words must be the basis of all teaching for the followers of Christ. Jesus, not the Pope, was the head of the church. These were the reasons why so much emphasis was placed on a simple and rational explanation of the Scriptures. At first, our reformation with its stress on simplicity rejected education; this was especially true of the Taborites and the Brethren. However, it soon became apparent that the intellect, too, could be enlisted as a weapon against Rome, and opposition to education was dropped. Eventually, Komenský became not only a bishop of the Bohemian Brethren but a teacher of the entire world.

The Taborites and later the Bohemian Brethren abolished priesthood and thus undermined the power of theocracy. They destroyed religious aristocratism in the conviction that from a religious point of view no man could be placed above any other. They understood that there could not be a double morality—a higher morality for the clergy and a lower morality for ordinary men. Thus, in place of spiritual and religious elitism they established a religious democracy. This attitude is also apparent from the Taborites' egalitarian acceptance of women as preachers and soldiers. And it was in the same spirit that the Taborites rejected the doctrine of transubstantiation.

In his *Síť víry* (*The Net of Faith*) Chelčický opposes both empires, the spiritual as well as the secular. He talks of two whales caught in the net: one is the Pope and the other the Emperor. This is how he expressed the inner connection between two kinds of absolutism, realizing that the church and state were only these two sides of the same institution. On the basis of this insight Chelčický taught that a religious man must never use violence. He rejected the violence of Žižka, of the Taborites, and of all other groups. It is true that our reformation ultimately led to violent struggle, and it cannot be denied that at times the Taborites resorted to more force than was absolutely necessary. But as Palacký correctly pointed out, the Czechs were fundamentally in a defensive rather than offensive position. We can see from Žižka's military regulations that even the harsh Taborites were aware that the war they were fighting was only legitimate to the extent that it was self-defense. It is moving to read in Žižka's writings how this hard-pressed commander remembered human concerns, even in the midst of many other cares. For example, he made special provisions for obtaining a warm quilt for an impoverished widow. Yes, our religious wars were essentially defensive, though I admit that we too were guilty of excesses.

Another striking feature of our reformation was its demand for justice. As the Taborite form of communism demonstrated, great emphasis was placed on political and social justice. Once again, this indicates that our struggles were aimed at reformation in the literal sense of the word and that its fundamental thrust was moral.

The moral impetus underlying our reformation movement is confirmed by historical analysis. It was formerly claimed that the reformation was above all a nationalistic one, and this view still has some adherents. There is no question that we defended our nationality against German inroads, but our struggle was principally directed against those Germans who supported Rome. Our sense of national identity at that time found its strongest and most characteristic expression in religious terms. If the issue had simply been a nationalistic one, the struggle would have taken a political rather than religious guise. It is also maintained that the Czech people was predisposed toward the reformation by its relatively high educational level. We know that a certain Roman prelate who visited our country during Hussite days stated that our peasant women knew the Bible better than most Roman prelates. Without a doubt, our university and contemporary schools were highly effective in propagating education among the people, and this cultural eminence was reflected in the Reformation movement. Only educated, thinking people could make use of the Bible as their sole religious authority. We may also assume that the high degree of order and tranquility prevailing in the Czech lands contrasted sharply with the chaotic situation obtaining in the German Empire, and this helped create dissatisfaction with Rome. Virtually all of these partial explanations of the causes of the Reformation point to a desire for a higher order of morality. The striving for a higher moral level, for a purer, more intense piety—this is the hallmark of our Czech Reformation. Certainly, we were further removed from the influence of Rome than the Germans and other nations. Some authorities maintain that lingering memories of the first Slavic missionaries, St. Cyril and St. Methodius, stirred a longing for a purer Christianity among our people. I do not share this view.

The entire Czech nation, as one single body, defied Rome; this is the special significance of the movement. Ultimately, of course, the Reformation spread all over Europe, but it took a century before other peoples followed in our footsteps. When Luther was accused of embarking on the road of the Czech heretics, he frankly proclaimed that he considered himself a Hussite and that all Protestants were in effect Hussites.

Now we must come to the heart of the matter. Why are we here, what do we want, what does the Reformation mean to us today? Are we here just to listen politely to a speaker—or are we troubled and stirred by Hus, is he still a living force in our lives? Did he die in vain, were the long, bloody Hussite wars in vain, were the bitter internal struggles in vain, the Reformation, the counterreformation? Thirty thousand Brethren families, the finest families in the land, were scattered abroad to fructify the German soil—was all this in vain? And consider the four centuries of our historical development, from Charles IV to Joseph II—is this long epoch of moral and spiritual travail without meaning? I ask you: if these four centuries truly represent the Czech spirit, the Czech character, our national religious outlook, is it possible for us to change and to live now in a different spirit? Is it at all possible? If we ponder these questions, we come to the conclusion that we would not be Czechs if we did not proceed in the direction and spirit of our reformation. It is all the more important for us to be aware of this truth as most of us are Catholics, in name or in reality. How can we resolve this dilemma? How can we belong to the Catholic church, yet acknowledge Hus as a national martyr, honor and revere him? My answer is this: Hus, the Taborites, Chelčický and Komenský gave us a better, a higher form of religion than was given to us by the Roman theocracy.

We see in the Czech Reformation a deeper manifestation of the Czech soul and of our national character. The Roman pontiff stated in his encyclical that our reformers were coarse, worldly men, whose god was their stomachs. I indignantly ask whether Hus, Chelčický, or Komenský were among the "libertines" scourged by the pontiff—a man notorious for his crudeness and lack of education. [Masaryk alludes here to Pope Pius X and his encyclical *Pascendigregis* (1907).] We were told that our reformers were not improvers but spoilers, we were told that they infected and seduced the entire world. Can we believe this? Do you honest Catholics believe this? Is it possible for a man to sacrifice his life in order to minister to his stomach? No!

Our people did not follow Hus for the sake of pleasure or material gain, but for the sake of the spirit, and we too wish to lead spiritual lives consonant with the Hussite example. We want to reestablish those sterling, shining qualities characteristic of our reformation. Just consider the courage of our Hussite ancestors, a courage possible only among firm, clear minds. Consider Žižka, a man of granite, reflect on his fortitude, his dauntlessness. A while ago, we listened to a hymn that exhorted us to disregard the overwhelming numbers of our enemies; this Hussite hymn is an expression of a faith that truly moves mountains. Consider Chelčický, Hus, Komenský—everywhere you will see firmness and determination carried to their limits. Think of the extreme devotion of Komenský, his fortitude, his deep thirst for enlightenment. Remember how Hus fought for truth, how he sang the praises of truth to his pupils and followers as if it were holy. And let us not forget the humaneness manifested even by the rough Taborites. Chelčický taught that violence must never be used, not even against enemies.

The Czech Reformation has truly outstanding religious aspects. It clearly demonstrated that religion is not only a matter of feeling but of reason as well. Hus and his pupils, Chelčický, the Brethren, Komenský, all longed to reach a higher form of religion through reason and education. Our reformation was predominantly nonmystical. It is not true that the basis of religion is necessarily mysticism, an intoxication with God. From the leaders of our reformation we get a desire for clarity, for reasonableness. Morality must be the decisive element in religion. Morality means the establishment of fraternal ties with one's fellows, it means energetic work for one's fellows; today, we would express it in terms of coming to grips with the social question. Further, we see that our religious striving was democratic, nonaristocratic; we see the anticlerical emphasis of our reformation. The movement was not directed at hounding priests but at eliminating and transcending the priesthood. It must be evident to all of us that in communicating with God no intermediary is necessary. Do you need servants, lackeys, and interpreters to talk to your own father? No! Either each one of us has direct contact with God, or he has none at all. He who hides behind an intermediary needs such a mediator out of fear, out of cowardice. I would say that the essence of Czech religiosity is quiet contemplation. Czech religion is not opposed to reason; religion without thought is useless. Then, too, as I have indicated, our reformation had a social character. Lastly, our reformation was marked by a strong manifestation of Czech national spirit; the Reformation struggles played a major part in forging our national consciousness, morally and religiously.

I have talked about the positive side of our reformation. But if history is to serve as a useful teacher, it must remind us of our errors as well. Every honest Czech should critically examine his own soul. We have our faults and shortcomings, and these were painfully evident in the course of our reformation. We tend to suffer from a certain vagueness of thought, a peculiar vacillation. Just think of Matěj of Janov and his recantation. Even Hus vacillated at the beginning, Jeroným recanted under pressure, before he finally decided to sacrifice his life. Even Mikuláš Pelhřimovský capitulated in the end to the weak Rokycana. After the death of Hus, great struggles raged for more than two decades. But in the end, the compacts were accepted and empty form triumphed over spirit. This may help explain how our own religious current finally became absorbed by the German Reformation; our own movement was not sufficiently strong, firm, determined. Our people fought to the death for a trivial matter—for the Chalice! Then, too, let us recognize our old Czech thick-headed stubborness. The compacts represented a shameful side of our reformation, yet we doggedly continued to fight for them for two centuries. The movement that began in the name of love ended as fratricidal hatred at Lipany. At the battle of Lipany, the Catholic and Protestant aristocracy allied itself against the democratic Taborites. Czech and foreigner joined forces to destroy those who were steadfastly dedicated to a renewal and cleansing of religion. We resorted to cruelty and violence on many occasions, even when it was not necessary; we were often aggressive in a provocative way. Our anticlericalism had a morally questionable side, when the church as a whole was blamed for the excesses of individual priests. Finally, the fanaticism that often emerged among the Hussites must be carefully distinguished from true courage and enthusiasm.

I believe that these shortcomings of our reformation reveal faults in the Czech character. It is, therefore, our task now to learn from history, to determine in what way we may best bring about a spiritual rebirth. Such revival must begin with individuals, only then can it become a rebirth of an entire people. We will be cleansed and rejuvenated only if we avoid the errors and safeguard the virtues that became manifest during our reformation. Let me put it this way: I am fond of Žižka, I sympathize with him, I find him an attractive figure—yet I must agree with Chelčický that the violence which Žižka used should be avoided. My model is Chelčický, a man as energetic as Žižka but free of violence. Hus attracts me by his example, but in the end I must admit that the Reformation progressed beyond Hus, and I choose Komenský. It thus seems to me that the present task of Czech men and women is to find a way of bridging Komenský and Chelčický. We must find the kind of harmony advocated by Komenský, a harmony that would unify all the beautiful elements of our reformation. I said harmony, not compromise. Not a compromise between Žižka and Chelčický, or between Hus and Komenský. Compromise is evil. Nor the golden mean for which Rokycana prayed! The way of the golden mean is the rockiest road of all.

I am not advocating that we should all revert to the past, that we should become Hussites or Bohemian Brethren. No, we must go forward, but in the direction indicated by our reformation. Of course, this means that *we must break our ties with Rome, not only in name, but in deed and spirit. We must overcome the Rome inside each one of us.*

Palacký stated that the emergence of the Brethren during our reformation represented the culminating point in the development of the Czech people, and he was right. We must therefore continue along this path. To use a grand word, we must feel our way into a kind of "congeniality" with our reformation, so as to discover those elements that are truly national and lasting.

I maintain that the national revival that began toward the end of the eighteenth century already contained certain elements derived from the Reformation. Men like Kollár, Palacký, Šafařík are direct descendants of the Bohemian Brethren, even from a purely religious viewpoint. Palacký stated that the ideals of Christianity found a culmination in the movement of the Bohemian Brethren. Shall this noble conception of the father of our country remain just an empty phrase? No, this is a living idea! Look at Havlíček. Can you fail to feel the motives of his struggle for enlightenment, for liberating humanity from the paralyzing effects of worldly absolutism? The struggle of our national revival to promote enlightenment is a continuation of our reformation, just as the French Revolution—from which we gained so much—was the continuation of the French Reformation temporarily halted by absolutism. The Revolution removed secular absolutism, it abolished Catholicism as the state religion. The American Constitution, imitated in Europe, grew directly out of the Reformation and the movement for religious freedom. A person who is free spiritually, a person enjoying religious freedom, will find his true political way. And conversely, political freedom facilitates religious freedom. As soon as we reach political liberty, our first act will be to accomplish the separation of church and state. Religion must be—as it was to Hus—a matter of conscience and not of politics.

Our political struggle often takes the superficial appearance of anticlericalism. *But our real task is to overcome Rome within ourselves, to bring about our moral rebirth.* The leaders of our reformation—whether from south or east, from Moravia or Slovakia—have but one message for us all, repeated and reechoed over our land: regenerate, reform the individual, regenerate, reform the whole people!

I can think of no better conclusion to these remarks than the well-known prayer of Hus. Let us heed it, let us heed it well: "Seek truth, listen to the truth, learn the truth, love the truth, speak the truth, keep the truth, defend the truth with your very life!"

 CHAPTER 2

The First Stirrings
of National Revival

*Our so-called "revival" toward the end of the eighteenth century,
connected with the European movement of liberation / Cultural
independence and our relation to German culture / The need for
philosophic orientation: German humanist philosophy / Through
German humanism Kollár forms historic links with Reformation
/ Kollár's and Herder's philosophies of history / Development
of language / A "philological" nation*

The European movement that brought about the French Revolution and resulting unrest had a profound influence on all Slavic
peoples, including our own. This movement coincided with the
beginning of our national revival.

Kollár grew to maturity during this crucial period. He was
born in the fateful year 1793. Thus, this apostle of rationalism and
humanism first saw the light of the world at the very moment
when the new cult of Reason was being proclaimed in the capital
of Europe. From his earliest years, Kollár breathed an atmosphere
of rebirth and renewal, and he continued to mature in this direction. German philosophy provided him with intellectual tools,

From Tomáš G. Masaryk, *Česká otázka: Snahy a tužby národního obrození*
(Prague, 1969), Chapter I.

[*15*]

while the movement of our national renascence helped to formulate his goals and to determine his field of activity. Herder, Fries, and other German teachers undoubtedly exerted a strong influence on Kollár. However, his ideas could not have emerged without the mighty, invigorating force of national reawakening, the yearning of the Slavic peoples for spiritual freedom and for the independence of their national languages. German philosophy alone would have been unable to define those noble and sublime aims to which Kollár pledged all his energies. No matter how skillfully wrought and well-designed a particular instrument may be, it is of little value without a leading purpose.

Let us clarify the needs and aspirations of that age. The new Czech movement had two tasks. The first was to forge a link with the past, with a period in which the nation still possessed its freedom and independence. The second was to gain a clear picture of contemporary circumstances, to become aware of the situation caused by national degeneration and to conceive plans and strategies for renewal. Comparison with other nations, comparison with their approaches to similar problems could serve as a helpful guide.

Our national awakeners had to determine what aspects of national life were still vital and worthy of preservation, what should be discarded, what should be adopted from others—it was a period of analysis, of studying both the past and the present. Depending on the scope and accuracy of these studies, goals for the future were based either on imagination or on reason.

Concretely, the main task was to create and nurture an independent, indigenous Czech culture, and to perfect the Czech language through many-sided literary activity. This was the positive aspect. From a negative viewpoint, the task was to counter the German linguistic and cultural preeminence and to resist German influences in general. We had to struggle against Germanization and to compete with our various ancient neighbors. Hungarian influences were less dangerous at that time, though they too had to be weathered. The close proximity of Slavic peoples—Poles, Russians, southern Slavs—still had only a negligible impact on us. The goal set by our awakeners a century ago is still valid for us today, and it will be valid for our descendants. Indeed, it is the persistent task of our people.

If we consider the extent of our decline toward the end of the eighteenth century, at a time when other nations—particularly the Germans—were making enormous strides forward, we can see what drastic measures were necessary for us to compete in the battle with German culture.

Our rural population retained its Czech language. However, the language was virtually lost by the intelligentsia; in the schools, the language of instruction was Latin, replaced by German in the eighteenth century. The counterreformation was conducted by our Habsburg rulers with such zeal that for several hundred years Czech efforts at literary and cultural activity were almost impossible. Tomek himself admits, "The Jesuits had imprisoned the Czech national spirit in a centuries-old tomb." It is often said that it was the rural people, the peasants, who have kept our national consciousness alive. This is true to some extent. However, none of the classes of the population had ever completely lost the consciousness of their Czech nationality. It was the job of our awakeners to gather all the dormant Czech forces together, to spark them to active life, and to nourish the flame of Czech culture that could successfully compete with its German rival.

Naturally, the enthusiastic struggle for revival and for cultural awakening had to be founded on a unified philosophical outlook. All mental work, all practical effort requires a clear and firm philosophical foundation. Otherwise, life would become but a series of isolated episodes, and no thoughtful, authentic person could tolerate such an existence. A philosophical perspective can take many forms, but every thinking individual must have an ultimate philosophic base.

Our awakeners, too, needed this foundation and discovered it in German philosophy. It is an irony of fate that German Philosophy provided the groundwork for an anti-German national movement. In order to build a Czech culture, our awakeners used German philosophy, and even French and English thought came to us primarily through German mediation.

This, then, is the historic significance of German enlightenment in so far as it served our awakeners toward the last part of the eighteenth century—men such as Dobrovský and Puchmajer. This, too, is the basis for Kollár's acceptance of the philosophy of Herder and Fries.

Enlightened, humanist philosophy was in perfect accord with

our yearning for progress and education. German philosophy and science thus repaid an old debt. The Czech Reformation movement had spilled over onto German soil and had fertilized it for the growth of new ideas. Thousands upon thousands of Czech exiles, the finest flower of a suppressed people, enriched German blood and German spirit. In its turn, the German philosophy of the eighteenth and nineteenth centuries repaid its debt to the Czech people and helped our awakeners rouse the nation from its long torpor. In a sense, the German, English, and French Enlightenment was a development and elaboration of the leading ideas of the Czech Reformation.

Czech thinkers after Kollár continued to derive their basic concepts from German philosophy. Palacký was indebted to Kant, Havlíček to Bolzano, Augustin Smetana and many others to Hegel, and more recently Herbart exerted a key influence.

In addition to philosophy and science, predominantly adopted from Germany, the study of history played a crucial part in the reestablishment of a national culture from the very beginning of our struggle. It was essential for our awakeners to learn the history of their own people, the role of the Czech people in human development had to be clearly defined.

Once again, a philosophical underpinning was necessary, and this was formulated most clearly by Kollár, utilizing Herder's philosophy of history. Before Palacký gave us a Czech history, we had a philosophy of world history, naturally once again adopted from the Germans. Palacký's history of the Czechs was preceded by Šafařík's work on Slavic antiquities. Our national consciousness thus gradually progressed from broad interest in abstract humanity to a sharper focus on Slavdom and finally on our own nation—as represented by the progression from Kollár to Šafařík and finally Palacký.

The development of our language followed an analogous pattern. Suddenly confronted with the complexity and multiplicity of modern life, the Czech language had to undergo not only purification but expansion as well. To replenish the vocabulary, our awakeners borrowed heavily from ancient Czech. Other sources included the related Slavic tongues, as well as dialects such as the Slovak.

Nevertheless, it was not possible for a language neglected for centuries to adapt itself overnight to the needs of modern intellectual life. That is why German continued to be used for scientific and scholarly work; Germanization was combatted through the German language. Dobrovský, of course, wrote exclusively in German; even Kollár still used German for his major works; Šafařík wrote in German about Slavic literature; and the first edition of Palacký's Czech history was published in German.

By placing so much emphasis upon linguistic rebirth, we became a "philological" nation, and Jungmann's dictionary assumed great national significance.

But the language did not develop only through scholarly philological study; literature played a major part in its growth as well. Language had to serve the needs of literary creation, prose and poetry. Here, too, the development was predetermined by conditions described earlier.

At first, our poets followed foreign examples, again primarily German. In his translation of Milton's *Paradise Lost*, Jungmann accumulated all the treasures of the new literary language. Translations were soon joined by collections of folk songs and imitations in the folk-song vein. In addition to Western models, Slavic literature as well as Czech folk poetry were utilized. Hanka published Serbian songs; Kollár, Šafařík, Čelakovský, and others collected indigenous folk music; and Čelakovský imitated Russian songs. Of highest importance, however, was Kollár's *Slávy dcera* (*Slava's Daughter*). It is no accident that our national ambitions were first expressed by a Slovak: linguistic consciousness remained purest in Slovakia.

During this period our poets were also involved in scholarship, while scholars engaged in belles lettres. This was true of Puchmajer, Hanka, Marek, Čelakovský, Kollár, Šafařík; even Palacký in the early part of his career composed poetry and devoted himself to esthetic problems. A sharp differentiation between scholarly and literary activity occurred only much later.

Finally, our national program of revival took the form of political struggle. The battles for freedom waged during the last decades of the eighteenth century sparked our cultural and linguistic renascence. This movement gained momentum, and the conception of our legitimate rights and political mission had become crystallized by the time the revolution of 1848 broke out.

There is no need to chart our further development at this point. Our present task is to elucidate the role of Kollár and his Slavic ideal in the overall movement toward national self-awareness. We shall describe and evaluate the various Czech and Slavic influences that were important to Kollár and to his immediate successors.

The question of religious and philosophic freedom / Josephinism / Dobrovský as an enlightener and forerunner of Kollár / Kollár, Šafařík, Palacký were all Protestants / Significance: continuity with ideals of Brethren

Our awakening, set in motion by the European movements of enlightenment and libertarianism, did not at once assume a consciously national form. At this time, particularly in Bohemia, nationality and language could not be regarded as concepts of central cultural significance. Europe had just gone through a social upheaval and a prolonged, materially and spiritually exhausting counterreformation. Under such conditions, fundamental religious and philosophical questions stood in the foreground. This is why the liberties granted by Joseph II and endorsed by the general trend of European thought had such great significance for Dobrovský as well as for our entire people. In view of the crucial importance that the period of reformation had in Czech history, religious freedom was especially significant and welcome to the Czechs. Religious liberty—even though still incomplete—was followed by national and linguistic liberation, in the same way that the reformation was followed by a strengthening of national consciousness and enhanced linguistic development.

At first, language and nationality were perceived merely as necessary tools of enlightenment. It was only later that the perfection of language and intensification of national awareness came to be regarded as valuable in their own right, as goals worthy of special political commitment.

The Czech movement that began in the latter part of the eighteenth century, in common with similar movements throughout Europe, was basically progressive, enlightened, and free-thinking in the true sense of the word. Josephinism was the official expression for this ideology in the Austrian lands.

Dobrovský, the leading figure of our revival, was himself a

Josephinist as well as a Freemason. Freemasonry was especially strong among the intellectuals. It is no accident that Dobrovský's first scholarly publication was concerned with combatting superstition. He demonstrated that a fragment of the Gospel of St. Mark, donated by Charles IV to the metropolitan cathedral, was not written by Mark himself. Anyone even slightly acquainted with Dobrovský's writings knows that the entire thrust of his thinking and scholarly work was marked by a passionate, enthusiastic, and thorough love of freedom. This was the source of his exemplary open-mindedness and his broad world outlook, without which his historical and literary work would have had considerably less influence. Dobrovský is not sufficiently well understood from this philosophic viewpoint. In some ways, he was too robust a spirit even for our awakeners, who found it difficult to free themselves from habitual modes of thought. Dobrovský's writings came alive only through the strength of his mind.

It is characteristic of Dobrovský that—like Kollár—he was a free-thinking priest. As a matter of fact, the majority of our awakeners were clergymen, to name only Dobrovský, Puchmajer, Marek, Dobner, Durych, Voigt, Vydra. Philosophy was cultivated almost exclusively by members of the clergy: Zahradník, Marek, Hyna, Klácel, Smetana. This is understandable, for in those days the clergy was still the major group of the intelligentsia, perhaps the only one; for this reason its contribution to our national movement was significant and beneficial. This contribution looms even larger when we recall that the pulpit was virtually the only school in which the mother tongue was taught.

This free thinking in Bohemia naturally had its roots in the Czech reformation, in the tradition of the Hussites and the Brethren. Our awakeners had resumed the development at the point where reaction had interrupted it. As soon as the small group of Brethren still remaining in Bohemia was granted tolerance, Komenský's *Labyrint světa* (*The Labyrinth of the World*) was among the first books to be published. The nature of the revival is clearly evident even in such details.

As we pointed out before, it is no coincidence that the first and the greatest among the leaders of the new Czech literary movement—in addition to the freethinking Dobrovský—were descendants of Bohemian Brethren and their Protestant followers: Kollár,

Šafařík, Palacký. These men were defenders of the liberty of conscience and of other noble traditions inherited from the Reformation, traditions that survived the onslaught of counterreformation Catholicism. Dobrovský, Kollár, Šafařík, Palacký, all proclaimed the ideals of humanity. Palacký revealed to us the true grandeur of our past as practiced by the Bohemian Brethren.

Significance of Kollár's humanism and enlightenment /
The right of our people to linguistic independence

The humanist idea of Kollár, therefore, had a clear historic significance. After the foregoing discussion, we can understand Kollár's intellectual development. We see that the ideas that Kollár encountered at the University of Jena had their roots in his own native land; that when he heard Fries and Harms lecture at Jena, he heard the voice of the Bohemian Brethren. We understand how and why Kollár was attracted by the humanist philosophy of Herder. From the ethical side—humanism; from the intellectual side—education. This was the crux of the national idea propounded by Kollár.

Our rights to nationhood and to our native language were legitimized on the basis of an enlightened humanism: no nation has a natural right to dominate another, no natural right can be invoked to prevent a nation from developing all its inherent potentialities.

These ideas were proclaimed by Dobrovský, Kollár, and Šafařík and were endorsed by Palacký. In his history of the Slavic languages and literatures Šafařík demonstrated that by his whole nature the Slav was "a true citizen of the world in the noblest sense of the word" who always fought for freedom and justice. The Slavs were eminently capable of "fulfilling the ideal of pure humanity." The freedom of the peace-loving Slavs and the progress of their literatures would prepare the way.

A similar idea was preached by Palacký in his history of the Czech nation. In his message to the Frankfurt Parliament of 1848, Palacký invoked universal humanism as a shield for protecting the Czech nation against German encroachment. He wrote: "In spite of my love for my own people, I honor human and scientific values above national values."

The emphasis on humanist enlightenment underlies all of our revival. This is the significance of the Učená Společnost (Learned Society), Matice Česká (Czech Literary Foundation), and other literary and scientific organizations that were founded during this period. Enlightenment philosophy was at the root of our concern for education, in the high tradition of the Bohemian Brethren. It must be admitted that through excessive rationalism Kollár weakened his effectiveness; nevertheless, it is as an enlightened humanist that he had the greatest impact on our evolution. His followers were satisfied to pay homage to his Slavicism, but for Kollár himself Slavic consciousness was but a corollary of a basic enlightenment philosophy. The shallowness of the rationalism of Puchmajer and his followers, culminating in contemporary liberalism, does not detract from the initial nobility and significance of the enlightenment outlook as it manifested itself in Dobrovský and his disciples.

Kollár and the so-called Slavic revival / Slavic evolution
similar to that of other groups / The "reciprocity" of European
peoples / Kollár's wish to enhance European collaboration
through Slavic solidarity

We have examined Kollár's basic philosophic thoughts in a historical perspective. We studied his ideals of humanity and enlightenment, and we saw the import of these ideals for our rebirth. Now, let us clarify the second fundamental idea of Kollár, that of nationalism, both Czech and Slovak. Kollár gave expression to the so-called Slavic revival.

In the true sense of the word, it was actually only we Czechs who underwent a rebirth, and it was our own renascence that gave its imprint to the entire Slavic movement. There was no corresponding phenomenon in Russia or Poland, except to the extent that the reform movement in both countries coincided with our own. The southern Slavs who were under Turkish domination freed themselves politically, while those under Austrian rule experienced a cultural rebirth only to a limited extent. No other Slavic nation manifested such deep political, social, and cultural change as we, and the national revival of the eighteenth century took its most remarkable form in our lands.

The revitalization and self-discovery of the Slavic peoples paralleled similar developments in other nations. For example, the Greeks underwent a renascence about the same time that we did. Above all, this was true of the Hungarians, whose evolution in many respects resembles ours.

The Slavs evolved by dint of their own resources, and to the degree that other nations emerged more rapidly, they benefited as well. For a long time now, the nations of Europe had ceased to be isolated. As far as the Slavs are concerned, they were always an integral part of the European Christian family and it is wrong to claim that a separation ever existed. This was not even true of the Russians, certainly not to the extent often claimed by various Slavic and non-Slavic thinkers and especially by nationalistic extremists.

Actually, the theory of Slavic separation from the European mainstream is no longer in repute, except in so far as it refers to a segment of the Serbs and Bulgarians. The Slavs were not isolated. The fact that they were often on hostile footing with other peoples, especially the Germans, is not an indication of isolation; quite the contrary. Furthermore, the Slavs had established numerous friendly or at least peaceful ties with the Germans and other European peoples.

The national awakening of the Slavs took place at a time when in France the rights of man were being proclaimed, when German philosophy and literature celebrated the ideal of humanity and when English philosophers were laying the groundwork for a natural humanist morality.

The idea of humanity did not stop before customs barriers and political border posts; on both sides of the borders, people yearned for the same goals of freedom and humaneness. In our country, these aspirations of European thought were in natural accord with the heritage of the Czech Reformation, and for this reason our rebirth represents a natural historical process and an integral part of the all-European development.

The proclamation of the rights of man was not limited to France, but applied to the entire Christian world and especially to our own nation. And when the revolution betrayed its principles and returned to the violent means against which it originally took up arms, then all Europe—including France herself—formed an anti-revolutionary alliance. The Holy Alliance formally codified the common principles that united the European peoples against aggressive revolution and against Napoleon. In Germany as well as in Russia, national sentiment rose against the European dictator. Of course, this alliance ultimately turned against the freedom of nations, but this constitutes another example—albeit a deplorable one—of European interaction and interdependence.

Literature and philosophy also provide us with evidence of common European patterns of thought and feeling. The leading ideas were the same everywhere; we Slavs took over the concepts worked out by our more advanced neighbors and distant colleagues. Voltaire wrote for all of Europe, and he was read in Paris, Berlin, Prague, and Petersburg. Rousseau expressed the longings of all peoples, and therefore Herder and later also Kant, Schelling, and Hegel became teachers not only for the Germans but also for us Slavs. Herder's humanist ideas live in Dobrovský and Kollár, they were invoked by Šafařík and Palacký. The message that Dobrovský and his followers wished to give the world was transmitted in a foreign tongue; through translation and rapid communication, the reciprocity of peoples and ideas was enhanced.

Byronism and Romanticism, dominant before and during the revolution, emerged again in full strength during the period of reaction. Byron, in particular, exerted a strong influence on us Slavs; consider Mácha, Mickiewicz, Pushkin. This is still another example of Pan-European literary unity and interdependence.

In this short space it is not possible to describe in detail the revival of all the Slavic nations and to compare their several experiences. But the account already presented suffices to justify the statement that the Slavic renascence coincided with the revival of other nations and that it had a general European significance. Change and development in the Slavic nations were accompanied by comparable transformations in other lands, both neighboring and distant. For example, the liberation of Serbia was brought about by the overthrow of Turkish rule, which in turn resulted in a basic shift in the entire political constellation of Europe. Similarly, the growth of Slavic literature, science, and philosophy created changes in European cultural attitudes and awareness, and these in turn influenced the further development of European social, political, and economic life. In effect, the cultured Slav was becoming more self-sufficient in all respects. The revival of the Slavs necessarily had a profound effect on European conditions. Kollár was well aware of this universality of the Slavic revival and expressed it by means of his idea of humanism and reciprocity. By calling for Slavic fraternal collaboration, he was asking for the kind of reciprocity that existed in much stronger form among other nations. Kollár wanted to enhance Pan-European collaboration by a greater intercourse among the Slavs. Of course, through Slavic literary interchange he also hoped to achieve a strengthening of national Slavic cultural life and self-awareness.

Universality of Slavic revival, confirmed by simultaneity of Czecho-Slovak doctrine of reciprocity, Polish messianism, Russian Slavophilism / Comparison of the teaching of Kollár, Mickiewicz, Kireyevsky

The universal significance of the Slavic revival is strikingly evident when we consider how the same Slavic ideal manifested itself simultaneously and independently in our lands, in Poland and in Russia, in Kollár, Mickiewicz, and Kireyevsky. The simultaneous appearance of the Czecho-Slovak teaching of reciprocity, Polish messianism, and Russian Slavophilism is in itself a strong indication that a phenomenon of wide-ranging significance was involved.

The teaching of all three Slavic thinkers was based upon attempts to solve the question of the historic destiny of humanity, to solve a fundamental question—how to arrange the life of all nations, of all human life in the best possible way. The Czech wanted to deal with this mystery through reliance on reason; enlightenment and humanism were to ensure the rationality of further human development, and all Slavs were to become the living embodiment of this abstract principle. The Pole attacked the same problem, but he emphasized feeling rather than reason; the problem would be solved not by enlightenment but by religion. The Catholic church and faith would provide the foundation for a movement whereby the Polish people in alliance with the French would become a leader of all nations. Since a new and definitive organization of numerous nations other than the Slavs was involved, Polish messianism must ally itself with the Pan-European movement. In fact, in the Polish view the Pan-European current had to be led into proper channels, primarily by France, which Mickiewicz regarded as the main source of European energy and power. Whereas Kollár—true to his humanist ideal—expected the achievement of his universal ideal through literary endeavor of all the Slavs, Mickiewicz expected fulfillment of his messianic plans through military victory. French power and military might, as revealed in Napoleon, were to serve the Polish ideal.

Kollár was one of the Bohemian Brethren, Mickiewicz was a Catholic after the heart of Boniface VIII, who supposedly held up two swords with the words: "Ecce due gladii, ego sum Caesar." The sword, then, was to bring about the Polish, Slavic human ideal. The sword was to unite the hostile brothers, Poles and Russians. The Czech hoped to unite those brothers by literary and cultural cooperation. In the Slavic heaven imagined by Kollár, arch-rivals and blood enemies were to be reconciled; Kościusko and Suvorov were to sit side by side in fraternal harmony.

Kireyevsky also attacked a universal human problem. Slavophilism was originally love for the Slavic church, for the Orthodox religion, and was only much later interpreted as love for Slavs. Slavic spirituality was to serve as a foundation for all government and culture, Slavic ideals could provide the basis for a Pan-Christian, universal organization. The light of salvation would shine in the East, Slavophilism would heal the split between East and West.

The similarities and differences among these three apostles of Slavic and universal love reflect specific national circumstances and current political situations. All have the same goal, but the methods differ. The Czech trusted science and philosophy, the Pole and the Russian turned to religion. The Czech expected salvation through peaceful, fraternal work, the Russian tended to agree, but the Pole reached for the sword. The Czech consulted reason but he granted the Russian that reason must be in harmony with the heart; the Pole appealed only to the heart.

Kollár: Among other peoples, there is a separation between head and heart; one faculty grows mighty at the expense of another. For the Slav, on the other hand, thinking and feeling are inseparable. *Kireyevsky*: Our goal is to merge all the individual parts of the soul into a single force, to find that inner center of being where reason and will and feeling and conscience, beauty, truth, desire, justice, mercy—everything encompassed by mind and heart—merge in a single living entity. *Mickiewicz*: It is not enough to know the real truth, we must be penetrated by its light and warmth. We must look into our hearts, for a world ruled exclusively by the head is an eternally tormented world.

Kollár: The life of mankind consists in the development of reason. *Kireyevsky*: Humanity, tired of the domination of abstract reason, longs for the wholeness of spiritual life, and such wholeness is only afforded by the Orthodox religion. *Mickiewicz*: I want to rule through the power of feeling, and the fount and guardian of emotion is the Catholic faith.

Kollár: The Slav will be the savior of humanity. *Kireyevsky*: The savior of humanity will be the Russian. *Mickiewicz*: Humanity will be saved by the Poles and the French.

Kollár: Let us find the common way through cooperation. *Mickiewicz*: The Polish nation has shown us the way. *Kireyevsky*: The way has already been pointed out by the Russian people.

Kollár: Let us trust the geniuses of all Slavdom—men such as Dobrovský, Kopitar, Šafařík, Gaj, Pogodin, Khomyakov, and many, many others. *Kireyevsky*: Follow the Russian muzhik. *Mickiewicz*: Let us be faithful to the genius of that great man, Napoleon.

A more detailed examination can be made by the reader himself. We will have an opportunity to compare and evaluate Slavic attitudes at a further point in this study, especially in our analysis of the messianism of Mickiewicz. For the moment, we only wish to point out that of the three Slavic leaders we have cited Kollár's ideas are the least specific. In particular, it is noteworthy that Kollár did not dare recommend his own people as the champion of Slavdom and of humanity, as the Russian had done. The Pole trusted only the help of a non-Slavic nation, the French. Napoleon was his messiah. Kireyevsky placed the Russian nation first only on the grounds that it had kept its Eastern orthodoxy in a pure form. Thus, all the three put their faith in universal ideas already in existence—humanism, Catholicism, orthodoxy.

The idea of nationality more firmly established / Humanism and nationalism / Herder, spokesman for nationalist principle / Kollár and Herder

At the same time that Kollár proclaimed the ideal of universal humanism, he annunciated the corollary ideal of nationality.

The idea of nationalism as it is now generally understood first began to establish itself in the second half of the eighteenth century, precisely in connection with the humanist ideal. Previously, people were conscious of their membership in a church or a state. But the idea that above and beyond church and state there was a nation, an entity with its own identity and cultural mission—this conviction penetrated to larger circles of the public only toward the end of the eighteenth century. We will not examine the various currents that contributed to this development. Suffice it to say that during this period, the nations throughout Europe began to liberate themselves in the name of humanism and natural right. Against the absolutism of Louis XIV, who maintained that he alone was the the state, Rousseau proclaimed that the state was the people, and the French parliament decreed accordingly. Herder was among the first, perhaps the very first, to formulate this philosophical position, which he derived from the humanist justification of the nationalist ideal. For Herder, the state was an artificial creation, for nature organized mankind into nations. Family evolves into tribe, tribe into nation; each nation, with its specific national characteristics, is a natural organization as contrasted to the artificial and arbitrary organizations represented by states. Wrote Herder: "Nature brings up families; the most natural state therefore consists of a *single* nation with a single national character. This character maintains its continuity for thousands of years, and is the most natural basis for educating people and ruler. A nation is a plant as natural as a family; it only has more branches. Nothing is therefore as alien to the purpose of government as the unnatural expansion of states, and the wild mingling of human races and peoples under a single scepter."

Herder drew from history the lesson and the hope that all artificial conglomerations of states would fall apart like pieces of clay, to be replaced by national states capable of realizing the ideals of humanism.

Kollár accepted nationhood as a natural organ of humanity, in accordance with the teaching of Herder and the underlying assumptions of Rousseau. In the name of humanism, Kollár therefore demanded freedom for his own nation and for Slavic nations in general. However, Kollár diverged from Herder's spirit in placing too great a stress upon nationality. He can be criticized for virtually losing sight of humanism, at least in his major work *Slávy dcera*, and for raising national aspirations to the point of national exclusiveness and chauvinism, and therefore also to the verge of injustice.

Slavic national consciousness / The main forms of Slavism:
Austro-Slavism, Russo-Slavism, Russophile Pan-Slavism,
Pan-Russism

The growth of national consciousness among the individual Slavic nations was quite naturally accompanied by growing mutual closeness. This rapprochement had several reasons. First of all, there was real awareness of kinship and linguistic affinity. Blood is not water, we are far closer to other Slavs than we are, for example, to Germanic or Latin peoples. Even from a purely practical viewpoint, it is far easier and quicker for us to learn a Slavic tongue than other languages. The Slavs tend to move closer to one another in response to the enmity of other nations, especially the Germans, who had at various times dominated the Slavs and lived among them. Some Slavs are linked by membership in a common political body. Finally, it was quite natural that the small Slavic nations would strive for aid from culturally and politically stronger Slavic allies. Kollár placed particular emphasis on this point and used it to explain why the idea of Slavic reciprocity was born in Slovakia—a relatively small and weak country.

Of course, the forces tending toward unification were countered by divisive tendencies. Slavs often complain that a propensity toward discord is an unfortunate part of their natural temperament. I do not know how true this is. After all, the Germanic Scandinavians have also found it difficult to unite, and the Pan-Scandinavian idea has failed in spite of German encouragement. Similarly, the Germans have long feuded among themselves, and politically they are still far from united. It is therefore not surprising that the individual Slavic peoples—influenced by differing linguistic, literary, cultural, religious, and political interests—failed to produce closer cooperation.

Except for the Russians, the Slavic nations are small and the majority live under Habsburg rule. For these reasons, from the very inception of Slavic awareness the Slavic question hinged on the nature of Austro-Russian relations.

In the Habsburg empire, Austro-Slavism was an inevitable fact of political life. In Budapest, and especially in Vienna, the Slavic intelligentsia was coming closer together within the context of Austro-Slavism. Kollár established intimate ties in Budapest with southern Slavs, and I believe that of all the Slavic tongues he was most adept at Serbian. Similarly, Šafařík established literary and linguistic relations with the Serbs. The Slavic political and geographic situation favored such rapprochement. The various nations encountered each other not only in the Hungarian capital but Slovaks lived alongside Serbs and Croats by virtue of their colonies in the south. In reality, Kollár's reciprocity became Slovak-Serbian and Slovak-Croat reciprocity. This was reciprocity in earnest, and in the year 1848 it led to political action.

At the same time, Russia was destined shortly to become the subject of wonder and longing for all Slavs, including the Poles. At the end of the eighteenth century Russia was the only independent Slavic state. Poland was defeated, Serbia gained independence only in the year 1815, only the Montenegrins enjoyed freedom. It was therefore natural that the Slavs turned their eyes toward Russia. Russia, however, was not only independent but a great power whose might was beginning to be felt throughout Europe. Prussia had always sought Russian friendship, and step by step Russia was proceeding to intervene in European affairs. To mention only one aspect of this involvement, Russia had become the natural protector of the orthodox southern Slavs by virtue of its age-old struggle against Turkey. The political influence of Russia was accompanied by ever-growing cultural and literary influence. It was therefore quite understandable that our awakeners studied the Russian language and literature before devoting themselves to the culture of the other Slavs.

The political and economic weakness of contemporary Austria had an important effect on our national awakeners. This weakness was dramatized by the disclosure of state bankruptcy in 1811. Our awakeners feared the onset of complete Austrian collapse. When Russia became the champion of oppressed peoples, fighting against

Napoleonic tyranny and imperialism, our leaders' hopes for the salvation of our nation and for the preservation of the newly awakened national consciousness turned to Russia.

Accordingly, Austroslavism was soon rivaled by Russo-Slavism, Russophile Pan-Slavism, or even Pan-Russism. We are about to embark upon a discussion of the development of Slavism in our lands, particularly in the pre-Kollár period. However, first we must examine Pan-Slavism and Pan-Russism as it manifested itself— of all places—in Germany.

Herder's Russophilism / Filangieri

Yes—before Kollár, and before our other Pan-Slavs, a definite and strong Russophilism emerged among the Germans. Herder, by birth a Prussian, anticipated Kollár in this respect, too. Kollár's teacher of the philosophy of history and of Slavdom was also among the first to propound the world mission of Russia.

Herder was born in 1744, and in 1764—right after the conclusion of his academic studies—he left for Riga, where he was active as a teacher and clergyman until 1769. This period proved to be extremely important for the development of his thought, especially his philosophy of history, and he himself considered his sojourn in Riga a most fortunate one. In particular, in Riga he had the opportunity to become acquainted with the post-Petrine reform movement, the ideas and plans of Catherine II whose famous *nakaz* (instruction) had an electrifying effect on him. He virtually deified Catherine in one of his odes and reveled in the majesty and grandeur of "Catherine's World," reaching from "the polar seas all the way to our lands (i.e., Riga), from China to the Baltic."

During his entire life, Herder regarded Peter the Great as an ideal ruler. He actually began his poetic career in 1762 with an anonymous ode on the coronation of Peter III. Herder's native soil was part of Russia for a number of years.

In Petrine reforms and in their continuation by Catherine, Herder saw an imposing attempt at educating a great nation. He believed her reforms to be motivated by humanist ideals, a view supported by Catherine's friendship with the French philosophers. He thought that through Catherine his own humanist ideals could be realized on a large scale. He was therefore preparing to write a work about Russian Enlightenment, hoping that this would stimulate the interest of the adored tsarina. He admired the Russians as a fresh, vigorous, unspoiled people. In contrast, on his trip to France in 1769 he verified with his own eyes Rousseau's contention that the French represented an old, decaying nation. Comparing the reality of France with that of Russia, or at least the Russia he knew from his Riga experience, he came to the conclusion that Russia could be converted into a highly original and remarkable nation (*Originalvolk*), reflecting the very paradigm of historical evolution. "The Ukraine will become a new Greece. This nation, with its beautiful climate, its cheerful naturalness, musical gifts, fertile soil, and countless other virtues, will shortly awaken. The Greeks, too, were once but a small and wild people. Similarly, out of many such peoples a strong and cultured Russia will arise, a nation whose borders will reach to the Black Sea and to the far corners of the world."

We will not describe Herder's enthusiasm for the Russian victories against the Turks, nor his disdain for his native Prussia (according to Herder, the Prussians will not be happy until their territory is broken up into tiny pieces.) Nor will we deal with Herder's view about Frederick's attitude toward German literature, and similar topics—the interested reader will easily find these matters in Herder's biography. Here, we are only concerned with stressing an aspect of Herder's thought which was so influential on our own development, namely the fact that Kollár's German teacher was not only a lover of the Slavs but an enthusiastic admirer of the Russians. It is also important to note that his views on Russia gradually evolved into the more general concepts regarding the Slavs and the future of mankind, presented in his *Ideen zur Philosophie der Geschichte der Menschheit* (*Ideas on the Philosophy of Human History*). In fact, the Slavs he knew were Russians; in the Russian, Herder thought he saw an incarnation of Rousseau's natural man. He considered the Russian aims to be representative of the historic mission of the Slavs, which would realize the ideals of humanism and enlightenment.

I do not know to what extent and by what means Herder actually became familiar with Slavic Russia. Judging by his writings, he was acquainted with historical books and journals, published to a large extent by German scholars then living in St. Petersburg.

Europe was quite knowledgeable about contemporary Russian affairs. Important works were published in German, Latin, and French, and Russian conditions were avidly followed throughout Europe. Even without a knowledge of Slavic languages, it was relatively easy for Herder to inform himself about the Slavs through the work of Slavic authors, writing at that time predominantly in German.

The growing influence of Russia and of Russian reforms, particularly those of Catherine, were noticed by other thinkers besides Herder. For example, the voice of the Italian philosopher Filangieri was an interesting one. Like Herder, Filangieri looked forward to Russian primacy in Europe. Anticipating an enlightened and humanist epoch, he saw a sufficient justification in the laws of Catherine II for Russia to rule over the degenerating nations of Europe.

Slavic consciousness as important part of the growing Czech national awareness / The beginnings of Slavistics / Slavic consciousness of our early poets / Puchmajer favored Austro-Slavism, yet he was strongly Russophile

For the reasons mentioned earlier, Slavic awareness grew among our people in proportion to the growth of Czech national awareness.

At first, around the turn of the eighteenth century, Slavic consciousness was nurtured by scholars, especially historians and grammarians. The work of such men as Dobner, Pelcl, Voigt, and Durych justified and reinforced not only Czech self-awareness but Slavic allegiance as well. Dobrovský became the focus of this movement. He was the great founder of Slavistics—he was a Slavicist before he was an expert on Czech studies. Slavistics is still used nowadays as a term denoting specialized Slavic studies. Scholarship has done more for our revival than many people in the so-called "practical," political circles realize.

The work of the historians and of Dobrovský soon penetrated into the awareness of the intelligentsia and the common people. Puchmajer and his poetic activity provide proof for this statement, in so far as poets rather than scholars may be said to characterize the thoughts and feelings of a society. Significantly, Puchmajer dedicated his *Sebrání básní a zpěvů* (*Collection of Songs and Ballads*) to Dobrovský, who had helped in the preparation of this important work marking the beginnings of our literary rebirth. It is true that the first volume of this almanac did not carry much Slavic emphasis. The introductory poem was Puchmajer's translation of an ode by Kheraskov, but the rest of the volume consisted of a motley collection of poems indiscriminately composed on German models and bearing little evidence of patriotic impulse. This is instructive and characteristic of the period. Only in the third volume (1798) did the poetry assume a more national character (for example, "Na Čechy"—"To the Czechs"), and reference was made to other Slavic peoples.

Puchmajer's effectiveness as a preacher of the Slavic message derived not only from his poetry, but principally from his involvement in the literature of other Slavs and his acquaintance with Slavic languages, especially Russian.

Puchmajer's most ambitious poem, "Chrám Gnidský" ("Temple of Cnidos," 1804) was modeled on the work of the Polish poet Szymanowski. In an interesting foreword, Puchmajer called for "the unification of all Slavs, at least those within our empire, through the use of Latin script." To this end, in order to bring Poles and Czechs together, he introduced his own orthography. He inveighed against the prejudiced idea that poetry flowered only in the West and not in the East, and he was convinced that a study of Slavic models would open "a rich vein of purest gold" to Czech poets. This was the only "certain way" of repelling the onslaught of de-Czechization and de-Slavicization. He especially recommended Polish poetry for its high quality. Translation from "foreign tongues" would be twice as easy by keeping a Polish version of the original close at hand. Furthermore, by becoming "more Slavic," there would be less danger that "our clumsy, Germanized Czech will ruin and confuse everything."

This, then, was Puchmajer's message: Slavic languages are needed in order to purify our own, and Slavic languages are readily accessible. Finally, it should be noted that Puchmajer favored Austro-Slavism, for the pragmatic reason that the Austrian Empire already included a number of Slavic peoples living side by side.

Neither Austro-Slavism nor appreciation of the poetry of "that unhappy Polish people" prevented Puchmajer from becoming a

Russophile. Our first poet also compiled the first Russian grammar. The connection between poetry and grammar was certainly quite significant for the time. Equally interesting was Puchmajer's dedication of his Russo-Czech Grammar (1805) to Růžička. Puchmajer was elated that, on his diplomatic mission to Kherson, Růžička was able to make himself understood to the Russians in Czech. He regarded this as proof that our neglected and despised Czech tongue could carry a man further in the world than other languages—especially, of course, German.

The final, fifth volume of Puchmajer's collection (1814) included Marek's poem "Jungmannovi" ("To Jungmann"), which already contained a clear Russophile call:

> From the East a Slavic spirit blows...
> For Rurik's sword is still in our grasp.
> And Moscow ever stands. . . .

However, before we turn to Marek and the second phase of our revival, we shall explore further the Slavic character of the initial period.

Dobrovský, founder of Slavistics, first herald of the Slavic idea / Humanism and Slavism / The Slavs as the light of humanity / Dobrovský a definite Russophile / His Austro-Slavism

Dobrovský was the spiritual center of this first period of national awakening. We described Dobrovský as an enlightened Josephinist, a disciple of the progressive Seibt, who revealed to his students the teaching of Rousseau and Hume—a real champion of humanist ideals.

Dobrovský as well as Herder and the Jena professors were all influential in leading Kollár to humanism, to Slavistics, and to the ideal of Slavic reciprocity. Dobrovský is the father of our Slavic consciousness. Kollár acknowledged Dobrovský as his principal teacher, and rightly so. Kollár only needed to extract rules and principles from Dobrovský's rich activity in order to have a ready-made framework for his Slavic edifice.

Kollár himself formulated his relationship to Dobrovský somewhat differently. According to Kollár, Dobrovský cleared the way for Slavic literary reciprocity, though "unconsciously and unwittingly." Dobrovský's writings were Pan-Slavic (*allslavisch*), "although he was not yet aware what such Slavic literary reciprocity really meant." And Kollár invoked the example of Dobrovský in trying to justify his own use of German when writing about matters of common importance to all Slavs. Dobrovský, too, had written his Pan-Slavic works in German or Latin, Kollár noted.

We have already indicated the significance of scholarly Slavistics founded by Dobrovský; our Czech consciousness was fundamentally a Slavic one. As the founder of Slavistics, Dobrovský was at the same time the first Bohemist, if we mean by that expression the sum total of studies concerned with the nature of the Czech people and Czech nationality. Dobrovský created comparative and historical Slavic and Czech grammar; he gave us the history of our literature still unsurpassed in the excellence of its conception and its profundity. Dobrovský made numerous historical and linguistic contributions. In short, he was a true pioneer in the scholarly exploration of the Slavs and of the Czechs. And how he penetrated to the very heart of his native language! He recognized the value of accentual verse in contrast to pseudoclassical quantitative verse; he codified the classification of Czech verbs—these two achievements in themselves constitute proof of Dobrovský's importance in paving the way for our national rebirth.

Dobrovský felt himself to be both a Slav and a Czech, or rather Czech and Slav.

Consider, for example, his pioneering publications *Slavín* and *Slovanka*, and you see at once how much Dobrovský achieved for the Slavic cause and how deep ran his Slavic sentiments. The introductory dedication of *Slavín*, "to our Slavic brothers," was very beautiful and profound. I mean that it was profoundly thought out and felt. Neither Kollár nor Jungmann, whose depth of feeling is universally recognized, wrote anything more warmly heartfelt. And how diligently Dobrovský searched through Slavic and world literature to find the most suitable material for illuminating the Slavic past and present! At the very beginning of *Slavín* he presented Herder's essay on the Slavs, with ant-like persistence he searched for anything that could further the understanding of the

Slavs and support for them. Similarly, in his *Literarisches Magazin*, in his *History of Czech Literature*—in short, in all of his works—he thought and felt like a Slav.

Dobrovský was a decided Russophile. His private lectures made it evident that he had made a thorough study of Russia and of the Russian language. He prepared a Russian grammar, and the Russian grammar of Puchmajer was dedicated to him. Kopitar accused him of being "half-Russian" and reproached him for excessive pro-Russian zeal. In one of his letters Dobrovský discussed the situation in Hungary, in which Hungarian was made an official language through the parliamentary decision of 1805: "The Slovaks are resisting this decision with great fervor. After all, if they really have to give up their own language, a better choice than Hungarian is available."

Dobrovský believed that Slavdom would illuminate the world with a new light. In a few lines, he wrote his whole philosophy of history. He opposed Kopitar's plan to found a Slavic academy in Vienna. He expressed his conviction that Vienna was not suitable for this purpose, because it was there that "the diabolic principle of Germanization was hatched." "The Germans may introduce improved methods and techniques, but it is the Slavs who are destined to bring a new enlightenment to the world. The Slavic 'um' ('mind') is the purest manifestation of reason in a deplorably corrupted humanity. German rationality merits respect, but it cannot compare to our 'um.' French esprit is volatile and can barely be grasped. *Qui potest capere, capiat.*"

Dobrovský also grasped the practical importance of the Slavic idea, and he surpassed his fellow countrymen in that regard as well. The details of the practical, political side of Dobrovský's activity will only come to light when a comprehensive work on Dobrovský becomes available. In Kopitar's letters the subject is only indirectly broached.

In this regard, Dobrovský's talents are well illustrated by an address that he delivered on 25 September 1791, under the auspices of the Learned Society before Emperor Leopold II. The address was entitled "On the Loyalty of Slavic peoples to the Austrian House." Because this address was so important for the history of Slavic thought as well as for practical political action, I will give a brief summary of its main ideas:

Dobrovský recalled the loyal attitude of the southern Slavs, and then showed that the Czechs had even greater reason than other nations for devotion to the ruling dynasty. The loyalty of the Czechs was demonstrated during the wars which were so destructive to Czech lands. Furthermore, the Czechs as well as the other Slavic peoples have played a big part in gaining glory for the imperial house, a glory that the might of the Slavs will continue to preserve.

After this introduction, Dobrovský pointed out to Leopold that his claims were not exaggerated. He pointed to statistics relating to the Slavic peoples. Step by step, he showed the contributions made by the Croats, the Slovenes, by Polish and Russian troops in Galicia and Lodomeria, by the Czechs, Moravians, and Slovaks in Hungary, and so on. In terms of numbers, the Slavs are at least equal to other nations of the realm. "It was the Slavs, with their might, who have helped to preserve the external security of the imperial house, and they have a right to take pride in this achievement."

Dobrovský then noted that the Slavs were once oppressed by Charlemagne and that later the Germans used the word "Slav" to mean "slave." Now, however, the Slavs are free and are helping to secure the power of the German emperor. Formerly the Slavs were exterminated in Saxony, Meissen, and other German lands. "Now, the Russo-Slavic race rules from the Black Sea to the Polar Sea, Slavs are signing treaties on the borders of the Chinese Empire, orders in the Slavic tongue are traveling over hundreds of miles, and Slavic ships are plying the oceans between Asia and America. In ancient times, under the Byzantine emperors in Constantinople, the Slavs had to toil like slaves to haul wood and to perform other menial tasks. Now, Slavs have taken the Crimea from the sultan, they have defeated his navy on the Black Sea. In fact, the Slavs—whose power and bravery are at your majesty's service—would have driven the enemy from his proud throne had not your majesty decided to end the bloodshed and to extend the magnanimous gift of peace to the vanquished foe."

After this Slavic part of the address, Dobrovský spoke specifically on behalf of the Czech people. The Czechs are loyal to their ruler not because they had learned from bitter experience that disloyalty is punished, but because they recognize their ruler as a just and wise lawgiver. Dobrovský ended his address with a plea to the emperor to protect the Czech language from "wild attack and extravagant coercion." It may seem advantageous to the state to have all subjects communicate in the same language, but on the other hand it is certain that all attempts at compulsion in this regard are harmful. All government officials in Bohemia and Moravia should know the Czech language.

I believe that now we can form a clear picture of Dobrovský's Slavic idea. Dobrovský considered himself genuinely a Slav. His Slavic sympathies were real and fervent. He took a logical approach to the Slavic concept, more logical and more consistent with humanist teaching than was the concept of Kollár. Like Kollár, Dobrovský was greatly affected by German Enlightenment philosophy. And as we mentioned earlier, Dobrovský was a sincere admirer of Russia. Our national Slavic consciousness had from the very beginning a decided Russophile coloration. This needs stressing, since it is a fact that certain Slavic writers prefer to overlook. At the same time, Dobrovský—like Puchmajer—also accepted the validity of Austro-Slavism. This is not surprising, in view of the practical political considerations that obtained at the end of the eighteenth century. It was only later that a pro-Russian attitude came to be regarded as necessarily antithetical to Austro-Slavism. In this regard, Dobrovský was well advised to listen not only to his Slavic heart but to his Slavic sense as well.

*Dobrovský's "doubts" about the viability of the Czech nation /
Similar attitude of Jungmann, Šafařík, Kollár / Dobrovský
a positive person; his honest and critical attitude toward the
Germans / Doubts of Dobrovský reflect recognition of our
small number*

Our characterization of Dobrovský would not be complete if we did not devote special attention to his doubts regarding the viability of the Czech nation. To this day, these doubts are casting a shadow over Dobrovský's memory. As in so many other matters relating to our history, this topic has been discussed only superficially and tendentiously. These are the relevant facts: First of all, Dobrovský expressed his skepticism honestly and openly. Who has the right to pronounce anathema over him in the name of a shallow, misguided patriotism? Dobrovský was misunderstood and wronged. His skepticism was more helpful to our rebirth and to the growth of Slavic awareness than the self-assurance of a dozen Hankas and other chauvinists of his stripe.

Even the widely acclaimed and glorified Jungmann had doubts, and this was after Dobrovský. As late as 1827, Jungmann wrote in a highly pessimistic vein: "It is our lot—Oh, how I hope I am wrong—to be the witnesses and abettors of the final destruction of our mother tongue."

Šafařík, too, doubted—and this much later still, near the very end of his life, as confirmed by Pypin.

Even Kollár doubted. Kampelík, in a passage from the year 1832, cited Kollár's statement: "Nothing will ever become of the Slovaks, nor of the Czechs and Moravians, if they remain isolated fragments. However, if they unite in a single body, if they band together in concord, if they act together, they will boldly withstand all the threats and attacks against their language and their nationality." Kollár's somber view is quite clearly expressed even in *Slávy dcera*:

> More than once it so appeared
> To my mind and aching heart:
> Eternal bondage was decreed
> Slavs are never to be free. . . .

On the other hand, it should be mentioned in this connection that in the year 1825 Palacký quite decisively countered the misgivings of Dobrovský and Count Caspar Sternberg, and made the memorable statement: "If all of us would take this attitude, then of course our nation must perish of spiritual hunger. But as for me, if I were of the Gypsy race and its very last descendant, I would still do my best to ensure that an honorable memory of my heritage remained in the history of mankind."

The fact that a number of our leaders wavered does not explain the significance of this phenomenon in our national rebirth. Let us examine further the skepticism of Dobrovský. It must be noted that Dobrovský's doubt regarding the future of our nation was not always the same and that at different times he expressed various degrees of anxiety. For example, let us look at a rather characteristic section of his *History of Literature* (end of the first edition,

1792). There he expressed himself quite positively and ended his work with a poem by Knobloch, entitled "Výstraha na hánce jazyka českého" ("Warning to the Detractors of the Czech Language"). There, we read: "Teuton, your speech is pleasing to me, but not more so than my own Czech. The Czech language should have its rightful place in its native land. Do not believe detractors! My language is not as bad as you may think, it adapts itself cleverly to everything, it can be given any form. Teuton, do not be so cruel as to take everything from me. Keep your own language and let me have the tongue of my ancestors; then our two languages can live peaceably side by side."

This probably reflects the opinion of Dobrovský, as early as 1792. It is a demand for *literary* equality. However, equal literary rights and equal literary worth cannot be secured by law-like political equality. Dobrovský and the writers who came after him simply had to accept reality. Dobrovský wrote in Latin and German, Šafařík published his *History of the Slavic Language and Literature* (1826) in German, Kollár used German for his tract on reciprocity (first ed. 1837, second ed. 1844). Even Palacký's *magnum opus* came out first in German (1836) and was published in Czech only in 1848.

Our greatest men—Dobrovský, Šafařík, Kollár, Palacký—wrote in German. Čelakovský was able to agitate for the Slavic idea in Prussia earlier than at home. In his *History*, Šafařík stated why he wrote in German: most of the material regarding the history of the Slavic language and literature was derived from German sources. There was an additional reason, namely "the wish to make the book equally accessible to students and friends of literature belonging to all the various peoples of our realm. I know from experience that differences in dialect, alphabet, and orthography between the various nationalities create a wall that hardly one scholar in a hundred has the desire and courage to penetrate. This admission, although sad, is unfortunately true."

German was enlisted as a weapon to combat Germanization. This means that during the period of the so-called awakening, nationality was not regarded from the viewpoint of language as definitely and exclusively as nowadays. This fact also reflected the degeneration of the Czech language; the Czech idea was at first not viewed as "nationalistically" as later. The same was true not only of the Czech idea but of the Slavic as well; as we saw, German culture and the German language had to serve in establishing the concept of Slavic identity and reciprocity. Dobrovský was familiar with numerous examples of Slavic scholars writing in German; this applied to Czech and Austrian scholars (such as Kopitar and others), and to Russians. Let us not forget that it was not only Dobrovský and our subsequent leading thinkers who availed themselves of German but that even the Russians had to turn to this language for scholarly and scientific purposes. During the period under discussion, Russian history was being written in Russia by Germans—Kohl, Bayer, Müller, Schlözer, Ewers, Raitz, Stritter. The Slavophile historian Bestuzhev-Ryumin even called Müller the father of Russian historiography. I am not saying that only non-Russians wrote Russian history or that men such as Tatishchev did not have great significance. The point is that during this time in Bohemia it was mainly the German authors who were generally known, as Šafařík had explicitly stated and as is evident from contemporary historical and literary works.

Thus, Dobrovský simply acted in accordance with the existing situation. There were two outstanding traits that characterized Dobrovský. He felt no enmity, no cultural envy toward the Germans, although he cursed "diabolical" Germanization. It therefore did not disturb him that the Germans might conceivably find a method for our Slavic Enlightenment. Such a way of thinking and feeling is typical of a man who not only has a great mind and heart but who is entirely *positive*, needing no hatred or envy to further his aims. Such people are always rare; the majority of people believe that loving one's own necessarily means hating the stranger. Dobrovský provided us with a shining example of broadmindedness. Under the conditions of sharp and unremitting struggle for the preservation of our language, such broadmindedness was not easy. Dobrovský was truly a humane Slav, an achievement that Kollár was unable to achieve in practice, no matter how earnestly he preached it in theory.

The harried followers of Dobrovský were often unable to understand and to value this calm, self-confident brand of patriotism. They were not capable of appreciating Dobrovský's strength, his truly Slavic strength. And so voices were raised which denounced Dobrovský as a traitor. It is bitter for me to have to admit that even Palacký, Šafařík and Jungmann took part in this "patriotic" campaign against Dobrovský. I am glad that Professor Král fixed the major blame on Jungmann. As a matter of fact, Jungmann often misunderstood our best and most honorable men, as we learn from Zelený's biography.

The positive attitude of Dobrovský, his "positiveness," is also related to his literary honesty and critical openness. This, too, many of our patriots—both new and old—fail to understand, as was painfully evident during the recent battles against the forged manuscripts. Dobrovský was among the first to challenge the forgers, and there, too, he played an exemplary part.

No small matter is at issue here.

In the battle of the intellect, as in physical combat, all honest means may be used. Manly, robust combatants always distinguish themselves through their chivalrous conduct; they fight courageously, openly, honestly. Only feeble spirits and poor soldiers take advantage of trickery and dishonorable methods. Dobrovský was a true knight of the spirit, and all dishonesty was abhorrent to him. That is why he assumed a critically watchful attitude. He was especially scornful of the insincerity and cowardice hiding under the banner of patriotism, which was just beginning to appear in our camp in his time and which we still have not succeeded in eradicating, much to our own detriment. It was a blessing that at the cradle of our rebirth stood a spirit as critical and honorable as Dobrovský to guide us and to lead our young generation.

Dobrovský deserves to be understood and followed, and I wish to do all I can to this end. It would be a sad judgment on our age if his efforts for the Czech and Slav cause were not fully recognized. What decent German would wish to denounce Goethe as a traitor? Today, even Frederick II is recognized by nationalistically minded people. Should we not pay homage to the man who was our spiritual father?

Let nobody think that I wish to ignore Dobrovský's skepticism. I do not deny it—he had real doubts about our future existence. But what was the nature of these doubts? Does not his tireless, enthusiastic labor speak for itself? Ordinary skepticism is incapable of productive work. But Dobrovský doubted the way a mother doubts over the cradle of her weak infant—and such anxiety, springing from the heart, gives rise to the dedicated work of salvation.

Only in this way can we understand the significance of Dobrovský's "doubts" regarding our revival and renewed Slavic consciousness.

These fears and qualms constituted the preconditions and major intellectual stimuli for the Czech and Slavic ideas. That is why Kollár decried our smallness in such fiery words; he did not dare hope that we Czechs would be able to survive on our own strength and our own resources. These doubts of Kollár's are but one facet of his Slavic idea. The same was true of Dobrovský. Only a later era succeeded in removing our misgivings, though we are still keenly aware of our smallness and insufficiency. Such knowledge will always rightfully induce in us the desire for interchange and collaboration with other nations, particularly the Slavs.

CHAPTER 3

Czechs and Slavs:
The Time of Kollár and Jungmar

The second phase of our national revival / The period of
Kollár and Jungmann (1810–1848)

The key figure of the second stage of our renascence—and its
most characteristic representative—was Kollár. Our remarks about
Kollár apply to a large extent to the whole period, which can be
approximately dated to begin with the publication of Jungmann's
translation of *Paradise Lost* (1811) and to end with the year 1848.

There was a rapid growth in the volume of scholarly work during this period, often at the expense of quality. In many cases an
unseemly hurry is evident which resulted in superficiality.

History and linguistic studies of course received major emphasis. Palacký became the leader and organizer of work in these
areas, and he strove with remarkable energy to satisfy the "spiritual hunger" of the people—a task that Dobrovský despaired of
fulfilling. At the start of this epoch Palacký was still preparing himself for his future role, and the task of advising and leading the
younger generation fell to Jungmann. Jungmann represented a
different facet of the mentality of this generation than did Kollár.

From Tomáš G. Masaryk, *Česká otázka: Snahy a tužby národního obrození*
(Prague, 1969), Chapter II.

[46]

Jungmann was an ardent disciple of Voltaire, an uncritical and blind adherent of Josephinism and of an old-fashioned kind of enlightenment. In this respect Jungmann compares quite unfavorably with Kollár, for Kollár—with all his rationalism—chose far better models to emulate. Jungmann even invoked Wieland, not only as a writer but as a philosopher! Jungmann was so consistent in his commitment to enlightenment that he even condoned absolutism, having in mind the Russian variety.

Jungmann provides a striking example of a particular tendency characteristic of contemporary literature. I mean precisely this Wielandism, the affinity of liberals for the superficial and ambiguously sensual piquancy of the French salons. Puchmajer had already translated Montesquieu's *Temple of Cnidos* (*The Spirit of Laws* was banned by the Austrian government). Later, Tablic and Palkovič demonstrated similar interests in Slovakia. Jungmann himself had strong leanings in this direction, and so did Hanka and others. Historically, Wielandism is readily compatible with Voltairism; Puchmajer showed the same verve whether he was celebrating Žižka or Venus. That the leading representatives of this current were clergymen only demonstrates how powerful an effect this foreign influence had on our awakeners.

Jungmann's diligence in inducing Marek to complete his work on logic and metaphysics is instructive in revealing another aspect of the epoch. Jungmann's concern stemmed from the fact that these disciplines had not yet been adequately treated in Czech, but it was also motivated by the correct assumption that scholarly activity must have a philosophical foundation and must be based on a coherent world outlook. Inveighing against German philosophy, Jungmann apparently felt the need for a philosophy of our own. But we were still quite far from approaching this goal; Palacký, Šafařík, Klácel, and others all depended heavily upon German philosophy.

In terms of its major thrust, philosophy still moved in a humanist direction. While Kollár proclaimed the humanism of Herder, Jungmann was closer to Voltaire, whose philosophy was also humanist and enlightened but in a manner not suitable for our needs. From his quiet retreat the forthright and sincere Bolzano also had a beneficent influence on our patriots; he was mistrusted by Jungmann but defended by Dobrovský. You always encounter

Dobrovský where hard work and goodness of heart are found. Bolzano, too, strove after humanist aims. But it was Kollár, nourished by the thinking of Herder, who really expressed what the time needed.

In addition to history, linguistics, and literary studies—such as the question of the value of folk poetry—natural science and mathematics were beginning to be intensively cultivated. Vydra's message exhorting the Czechs to excel in mathematics did not fall on deaf ears. The first technical schools were founded in Prague, with instruction still carried out in German. But the studies that were truly "national" par excellence were political and literary history and linguistics, in other words, Slavistics in the broadest sense of the term. The mind of the researchers was always turned to the distant past; only indirect attention was paid to the present. This approach, which may be characterized as "archeological"—Kollár's historicism, Šafařík's antiquities—was quite general.

During this period, the most "modern" figure was Čelakovský. He absorbed himself in folklore and folk music, esthetic and philosophic sensibility. Čelakovský published his collections of national songs in the years 1822 through 1827, *The Echo of Russian Songs* in 1829, *The Echo of Czech Songs* in 1840, and *The Wisdom of the Slavs* in 1852.

Šafařík as a Slavicist / Slavistics preceded Czech studies / Logical relation between general and specialized knowledge

After Dobrovský, work in Slavistics was continued by Šafařík, principally focusing on the history of the old Slavs. Dobrovský's Slavic grammar was followed by Šafařík's *Slavic Antiquities*.

It is time to make a remark which I believe to be important for the evaluation of national consciousness. It is not accidental that the investigation of our own Czech history and Czech language was preceded by a study of the history, literature, and language of the old Slavs. Why did we first have *Slavic Antiquities* before we had *History of the Czech Nation* (1866), why was the *Old Czech Grammar* (1845) preceded by the *Institutiones*?

In order to pursue a specific field—in our case, Czech national and linguistic history—a general conceptual basis is necessary. This is why Kollár as well as the other awakeners turned to German philosophy, particularly German philosophy of history, and for the same reason specific Czech problems were placed within a larger Slavic framework. It was also necessary to have a general focus and orientation. The delineation of Czech national existence required continual comparison with the existence of other Slavic nations. Therefore, Slavistics quite naturally preceded Bohemistics, and our national Czech consciousness had to pattern itself upon Slavic consciousness. Our Slavic heritage also provided a suitable basis for scientific research and thought.

There was still another objective, philological reason for this relationship between Slavic and Czech studies. We shall discuss it later, in connection with the question of a unified literary language.

"Slav and Patriot" / The abstract essence of Slavdom / Ignorance of true Slavic existence / Disputes about the manuscripts / Misuse of Slavic analogy in Czech history

"Slav and Patriot"—that was the slogan of contemporary Slavic sensibility formulated as early as 1810 by Jungmann.

Even though the national movement was founded on deeper conceptual principles, the struggle for a pure Slavic language was the main demand of the time. Kollár is characteristic in this respect. His work had two facets: a Herderian-humanist one, and a purely nationalistic one as expressed in *Slávy dcera*. This epoch marks the beginning of the dominance of the word—or, to enter into the contemporary spirit—the "tsardom of the word." "What *language* has joined, let no man tear asunder," preached Marek. For our tongue is *holy*, exulted Kollár. Such dedication to language explains the intensity and bitterness of contemporary disputes over relatively trivial orthographic and lexical questions.

Yet, in spite of all this fervor, Slavic awareness was still rather abstract. Let us examine the matter a bit more closely.

Of course, people who judge a period only by its slogans and pious wishes will be quite satisfied with our Slavic attitudes of the time, as well as with the current state of affairs. But people who are in the habit of judging on the basis of deeds, people who search into the true motives and causes of action, will get quite a different impression. Not everyone who mouths the name of the Lord will reach the heavenly kingdom.

In spite of all the enthusiasm for the Russians and for other Slavic brethren, and in spite of all the opposition to the Germans, it was the Germans who continued to act as our true teachers. Jungmann and Marek, Čelakovský, Vocel, and others remained just as dependent upon German ideas as was Kollár. Just as Kollár drew his main ideas from Herder, so Marek—that sincere Slav and Russophile—in his struggle to establish a Czech philosophy gave us Czech versions of the Kantians Kiesewetter and Krug. Even the disputes about prosody and about the anti-Czech prejudice of Dobrovský's opponents were inspired by German classicism and German poets such as Klopstock and Voss, who favored the poetic forms af antiquity.

And yet Russian and Polish literature could have provided the kinds of models that our poets and writers sought in German. In the 1830s and 1840s we could have read and studied Krylov, Griboyedov, Zhukovsky, Batyushkov, Yazykov, Pushkin, Lermontov, Gogol—where are the influences of that literature? Where is the philosophic influence of Chaadayev and Kireyevsky, Mickiewicz, Krasiński?

Needless to say, I am well aware that there were—and continue to be—valid reasons for our dependence on German culture. My aim is merely to point out the facts and to demonstrate how far we still are from fulfilling our own demands. From the very beginning, our Slavicism contained much that was distorted, superficial, and morbidly unrealistic. Mere words were mistaken for Slavic sentiment, mere assertions for the truth. It was certainly useful and necessary to borrow expressions from other Slavic tongues, as Jungmann had done in his translation of *Paradise Lost.* But what Jungmann, Šafařík, and Kollár had done with full awareness and understanding, lesser men did merely out of a desire for modish imitation.

With respect to Jungmann's translation of Milton, I have another remark to make. There is no question that by means of this work Jungmann helped create our literary language; but is it not strange that the subject matter of this poem is non-Slavic? True, it was not German—I have remarked some time ago regarding the beneficial effect of English literature on our development. To a large extent, the English have provided the subject matter for our literature, the Slavs the form. When will the content and ideas of our works become Slavic, too?

Our fancifulness, dilettantism, and inability to distinguish critically Old Czech from New Czech and our own literary products from those of fellow Slavs became painfully evident in the course of the disputes about the forged manuscripts. The nature of contemporary Slavicism was revealed in its true protean form.

From a purely scholarly viewpoint a knowledge of the Slavic world was urgently needed. On the other hand, such knowledge was misused and a false analogy with the experience of fellow Slavs often resulted in a distorted understanding of our own existence. The idea that we had ever completely lost our Slavic character was quite superficial and exaggerated; in many ways, the nightmares that our awakeners conjured up receded in the light of day. One typical example concerns Palacký's *History*. In reconstructing our distant past, Palacký accepted too uncritically contemporary opinions about early Slavic identity; for example, the concept of the communal nature of early Slavic life won wide acceptance, and by analogy our Czech forefathers were automatically assumed to have led a communal existence. Similarly, nobody raised the question of whether contemporary south Slavic communes had always existed in their present form, or whether they had gradually evolved in the manner characteristic of other social entities. Such problems were not even discussed.

The question of a unified literary language

Deliberations on an all-Slavic language, a single unified literary tongue, also reveal the unreality and fancifulness of contemporary thought. However, the question also has its more serious side.

Nowadays, it is self-evident that no literary language can be artificially constructed. The idea of a Slavic *volapük* cannot be taken seriously by anyone. But the matter seemed more attractive to our forefathers, for in their time our own literary language was just beginning to take definitive form, and lexical borrowing from other Slavic tongues was common. It is therefore no wonder that Dobrovský, Puchmajer, Jungmann, Šafařík, Kollár, and of course

Hanka diligently pondered the possibility of a single all-Slavic language. Šafařík, for example, expected that national and linguistic peculiarities were on the wane and would soon disappear.

Others held similar opinions, but in order to make a generalized statement we would have to know specifically how each of our leading men envisioned the origin and essence of the artificial language. We would need to know, for example, whether Dobrovský was thinking in terms of a liturgical language. These matters were treated in a voluminous work recently published by Budilovich. He propounds a thesis that has now become virtually self-evident, namely, that Russian constitutes the only feasible language that the Slavs could utilize as a basis for a common literary means of expression.

These deliberations had not only a national and political significance but a scientific, linguistic one as well. Philology was becoming transformed into comparative philology, engaged in finding and constructing common linguistic categories and in reconstructing a common protolanguage. In this sense, Slavic linguistics had actually arrived at a common unified tongue.

Polophilism / Polish uprisings of 1830 and 1863 / Russophilism / "Hanka's party" / Antonín Marek

We accused Kollár of having been a "Slav in abstracto." The same accusation could be leveled against the entire epoch. When Jungmann learned of the rumor that the Czech lands were about to be joined with Galicia, he was pleased and remarked that he did not mind if the official language became Polish, as long as it was Slavic. But Jungmann's attitude was mistaken, and demonstrates the bookish, abstract quality of contemporary Slavism.

Since I have already mentioned the Poles, we may as well examine the Polophilism that existed in our lands at that time.

We have remarked that Puchmajer had drawn upon the Polish language and literature, while recommending Austro-Slavism—and while remaining a staunch Russophile. Earlier, the attitude of Dobrovský regarding the Poles can be judged from the articles on Poland which he gathered in his literary publications; these articles are still instructive today.

The uprisings of 1830 and 1863 gave fresh impetus to our Slavic patriots' involvement in the Polish question. We know from the correspondence between Jungmann and Marek that a pro-Polish party had come into existence. Marek himself was not an adherent; on the contrary, he rejected the *Dziady* (*The Forefathers*) of Mickiewicz. There is no doubt that during this period the study of Polish was gaining momentum among our people. This is confirmed by Šafařík's study of Polish authors such as Surowiecki, as well as the use of Polish sources by Kollár and many others. The influence of Polish literature was especially marked in Slovakia. Slovak youth enthusiastically supported the Polish cause in 1830, and Samo Chalupka came home from the uprising with a wound. Čelakovský, long an outspoken Russophile, was removed from his post at the request of the Russian ambassador to Vienna after he had condemned Russian reprisals against the Poles. Such episodes certainly speak well for our dedication to freedom. The younger generation, too, did its part on behalf of the Poles, during the second uprising in 1863.

The Russo-Polish dispute cannot be dismissed with a few words. For the moment suffice it to say that our lack of sympathy with the backward aristocratic-clerical leadership of Poland was certainly justified. The Poles interpret our Russophile attitude incorrectly, they see in it mere homage to physical might, as Mickiewicz chided Kollár. The Czech senses in Russian literature, Russian thought, and life a kindred intellectual and spiritual force that warms and strengthens him. Actually, shortly after the first uprising even some Poles themselves had pro-Russian sympathies, Gurowski for example. And does the present generation of Poles still fail to understand the true nature of the improvisations of Mickiewicz?

Our Slavic patriots established close personal ties with leading figures of other Slavic nations within the Austrian Empire as well as with Russians. Russia, as the head of the Holy Alliance and the logical foe of French revolutionary expansionism and Caesarism, won the confidence of the Czech people and the Western European nations. The establishment of chairs of Slavic studies at German and French universities is an indication of the growing attention that the Slavic movement received in the West.

The Slavic idea was perceived from the very beginning mainly with Russia in mind. Jakub Malý, referring to the influence of

Kollár's *Slávy dcera*, wrote: "At this time—the time of Kollár—our individual national identity was so questionable as to hold out little hope for the future. But at least our nation had the hope of preserving its Slavic character as a member of an entity eighty-million strong." Malý discussed the origin of the Russophile party, which regarded Russia as the natural protector of all oppressed Slavs. He noted that "feverish minds" propagated the idea of a mighty Slavic federation, and this idea—nurtured in Russia by secret societies—led there to the uprising against Czar Nicholas in 1825. "These aspirations were quite common in Bohemia, awakening in sanguine temperaments premature and extravagant hopes.... But to the honor of Czech common sense it must be added that the 'Russian party' among the patriots—whose soul was the late Hanka —was quite small compared to the great majority who saw our nation's salvation only in its own efforts... in its assiduousness and determined adherence to its chosen path leading to spiritual rebirth and ultimately also to material emancipation."

Malý put his finger on one reason for our Russophilism. The small size and relative weakness of our nation were to be compensated by a power that was foreign but ethnically related. Malý was wrong, however, in his belief that the greatness of Russia was universally perceived only in physical terms. In the aforementioned address to the emperor, Dobrovský proclaimed Russia as the representative of all Slavs, and surely nobody would accuse Dobrovský of materialism.

Kollár, too, stated quite clearly and definitely why it was Slovakia that gave birth to the ideal of Slavic reciprocity. "Whoever possesses a great deal is usually satisfied with what he has and has no wish to expand. But he who has nothing wants a great deal, wants everything. The Carpathian Slovaks have had no literature of their own; this is why they were eager to spread their arms and to embrace all Slavdom."

It is true that Hanka conceived of Russophilism in a rather materialistic and petty way, getting his scholarly Slavic information in the form of crumbs falling off the rich table of Dobrovský. But it would be unfair to claim that during this particular period only the Hankas were pro-Slavic and pro-Russian. For example, Marek —whose message about Jungmann has already been cited—was an entirely different breed of man. Marek envisaged the Slavic idea much more profoundly than Hanka or Jungmann, and in a far more logical and consistent way.

Light and shadow

The picture of the period would not be complete if we did not devote at least a few lines to the moral character of the contemporary figures.

The positive side is frequently paraded before our eyes, and rightfully so: devotion and love for the native land, enthusiasm for the national cause, indefatigable industry and self-sacrifice—these are certainly beautiful and ennobling qualities. But the picture is not without its shadows, some of which are quite dark indeed. We were recovering from spiritual and political subjugation, and we did not discard our fetters all at once and forever. No sooner had Emperor Joseph eased Austrian rule than a new wave of reaction swept back, and it was a petty, harsh reaction. Even the Germans were forced to submit to severe reactionary rule, but we and the other Slavs suffered most. This damaged character and candor among our people. We can judge how sad a time it was from Zelený's assertion that Jungmann concealed his deepest convictions even from his most intimate friends!

In a small nation there is special danger that prudence degenerate into duplicity and unmanly lassitude. External slavery induces inner slavery, and dishonorable means are adopted by feeble individuals believing that they are serving their country. This happened in our country. Literary shabbiness and deception slowed our scholarly and scientific development. Our social and political progress was impeded by a lack of directness and manliness and a propensity toward a particular kind of fantasticality. Such lack of realism generally has roots that are not only intellectual but, perhaps above all, moral.

Kollár as a product of his epoch and its main representative / Foreign influences; Herder and his effect on Czech thinkers and on other Slavs

Kollár was the principal representative of this period. Only now, in retrospect, can we see his Slavic idea in its full historical light.

Now we can not only evaluate foreign influences, particularly German, but domestic ones as well.

With the help of German philosophy, Kollár explained the world-historical significance of the Slavic revival. This seminal influence on Kollár and a host of other Slavic thinkers was especially exerted by Herder. Herder's philosophy gave Kollár the necessary foundation for his Slavic idea. Herder formulated the concept of the historic mission of the Slavs and he was even the forerunner of Kollár's Russophilism. Herder led our awakeners to the study of national folk culture. I believe that this aspect of Herder's contribution is now fully recognized. Let us remember that Herder exerted his effect throughout the Slavic world, and the striving of various Slavic thinkers therefore received a unified philosophical and sociological foundation. Herder's ideas—not only on the Slavs but on various philosophical questions as well as on folk poetry—were accepted by Dobrovský, Šafařík, Jungmann, Čelakovský, Palacký, and later by Štúr. All of these men acknowledged their indebtedness to Herder and translated parts of his works.

In Poland, Herder had a clearly evident influence on Surowiecki, who in turn had a direct effect on Šafařík. Herder's impact was particularly strong in the case of Brodziński, the Polish apostle of the idea of pure humanism. Brodziński soon became known to several of our leading figures, including Čelakovský.

In Russia, Herder was well known to Karamzin and Nadezhdin. The literary-historical works of the Slavophile Shevyrev owe a great deal to Herder. Maksimovich and Metlinsky, collectors of folk songs, also came under the influence of the German philosopher.

In brief, Herder was the main teacher of the Slavs during their period of renascence.

Of the Slavic influences stimulating Kollár, the strongest impact was of course exerted by Czech culture. Dobrovský, and more especially the younger generation under the leadership of Jungmann and Šafařík, had the most lively impact on Kollár. His debt to Šafařík was especially notable, as he freely admitted in his work on Slavic reciprocity. The influence of Šafařík must have been all the more significant in view of the common philosophic and scholarly background that the two men received in Jena. Šafařík was in Jena just before Kollár and was subject to the same philosophical and social currents that impressed Kollár. For example, Šafařík studied under the same professors: Fries, Oken, Luden. Furthermore, both were Slovaks. It is therefore understandable that Kollár felt a special affinity for Šafařík, that he was guided by his scholarly works, and that the two men cooperated in publishing Slovak folk songs.

Kollár often cited Kopitar, too, and was in close touch with him. He also maintained contact with other contemporary Slavic writers, but this is beyond the scope of our study. We should mention that the influence of Slavic authors writing in their own national tongues was quite limited. In the year 1844, when the second edition of Kollár's book on reciprocity was published, Kollár was apparently unaware of the contributions of certain Russian authors which were highly significant to his topic. It may be said in Kollár's defense, however, that these authors are still somewhat obscure even today. In *Slávy dcera*, Kollár cited Khomyakov for his poem "Orel," but in general Kollár was unacquainted with the Slavophile and Westernizing tendencies in contemporary Russian literature.

These, then, were some of the major currents that affected the genesis of Kollár's Slavic ideas. Our understanding of these sources will be enriched by future studies examining Kollár not only as an apostle of the Slavic idea but as a writer and poet.

Significance of the Slovaks for our revival / Slovaks preserved their language / Slovaks and their relation to other Slavs / Kollár as a humanist citizen of the world

Kollár was a Slovak, he lived and worked in Slovakia, far removed from Prague. This is a matter that deserves special consideration. Kollár himself declared that the idea of Slavic reciprocity arose in Slovakia, and he explained why: through reciprocity, ethnic limitations were transcended. As he told Kampelík, without ties to other Slavs "nothing could be expected," neither from the Slovaks nor from the Czechs. Slovak and Czech skepticism was to be cured by faith in Slavdom.

It is certainly noteworthy that a Slovak became the first prophet of the Slavic idea. This deserves much thought, and the Slovak question in general is of the greatest significance for us. It is high time for us to do more than sing Slovak folk songs—though even that is gradually being forgotten—but to feel Slovak and to think Slovak. Yes, to think; that is what Kollár's seminal work asks of us, Slovaks and Czechs alike.

Strange circumstances of our revival! Our first awakener was a Czech born in Hungary. He woke us with a voice that was mighty but foreign—we responded to its spirit, reasonableness, and warmth. The hymn celebrating our rebirth was sung by a Slovak, and another Slovak presented us with the magnificent past of the Slavs as a model for our own national striving. A Moravian painted the picture of our ancient history for us, and finally it was a Czech who gathered us all together into a mighty camp of patriots. Dobrovský–Kollár–Šafařík–Palacký–Havlíček.

Slovaks gave a home to our exiles in times of trouble, and in their spirit worked for our mutual rebirth. In Kollár's words we hear an echo of the voice of our ancestors. In Slovakia, our language has survived in a purer—albeit dialectical—form, and that is why the first mighty Czech song was sounded by a Slovak. Everything that Czech literature owes to Kollár, and it is a great deal, stems from Kollár's Slovak origins.

In the Slovak people, Kollár was able to observe those sterling qualities that Herder ascribed to all the Slavs. There may be some question as to whether Kollár's characterization of the Slavs truly reflects reality. But I have no doubt whatever that Kollár genuinely perceived the good qualities of the Slavic people and that his portrayal of the Slavs reflects a good likeness of contemporary Slovaks. The particular piety, industriousness, innocent gaiety, love for the native language, and finally the peace-loving tolerance —qualities that Kollár attributes to all the Slavs—are certainly typical traits of today's Slovaks. Of course, Kollár was not sufficiently familiar with all the Slav peoples, and so he naturally generalized the experiences of his own immediate surroundings.

Even the geographic location of Slovakia played an important part during the revival. Kollár himself pointed out that Slovakia was the heartland of the Slavs and that the idea of Slavic reciprocity had its natural origin there. True, Kollár is taking poetic license.

But the fact remains that Slovakia borders on territories occupied by Poles, Russians, and southern Slavs. Slovaks have intimate contact with other Slavs, for example with the Russians living in Hungary. The Slovak and Russian languages overlap, one merging into the other. As far as Russian influence is concerned, it is significant that Kollár came from a region whose inhabitants have long been in the habit of traveling to Russia in the course of their work. I myself have witnessed many occasions of Russification of simple Slovak tradesmen. Kollár's mother, as Kollár recalled in his memoirs, came from a family that pursued its trade in Russia. We can read in the memoirs that Russian soldiers marching against the Turks made a deep impression on young Kollár. He was especially impressed by a Cossack named Ivan Danilov. Through a remarkable coincidence Danilov later became Kollár's teacher of Russian in Jena.

We already had occasion to note the influence of Serbs and Croats. Kollár associated with Serbs and Croats in Pest and thus really practiced Slavic reciprocity.

The widespread travel and emigration of Slovaks necessitated by the poverty of their land was not without relevance to mutual Slavic acquaintance. The proverbial Slovak "itinerant tinker" was but one example of involuntary Slovak world citizenship. Kollár's humanism and universal outlook had a connection with such poor but hard-working and honorable world travelers, ultimately returning to their native village after experience with many languages and cultures.

And let us remember that Kollár's Slavic sensibility was also colored by the contemporary domination of the Slovaks by Hungarians. The Slovaks found Hungarian oppression especially galling as there was no justification for it except brute strength. The Germans were able to awe us with their literature and numbers, but this was not true in the case of the Hungarians. The cultural level of the Hungarian people was even lower than that of the Slovaks; the Hungarians had no literature in Kollár's day, nor do they have an important literature even now. The tyranny over the Slovaks had a purely physical basis, and for that reason denationalization and Magyarization had such disastrous cultural and moral consequences.

Kollár, describing the struggle between Germans and Slavs, is unconsciously echoing the unfortunate conflict between Slovaks and Hungarians. This is the reason why Kollár's imagery of denationalization is so rich and convincing. In contemporary Bohemia and Moravia the scenes of oppression described by Kollár had long faded from memory. In contrast, the Hungarian dominance was present and real and was felt all the more bitterly because the Hungarians were themselves still striving to perfect and enlarge their literature and their language.

Professor Sobyestiansky opposed to sentimentalization of ancient Slavic character / Slavs were not passive and mild, but enterprising, aggressive, and cruel / The idealization of Slavs politically motivated / Wrong evaluation of ancient Slavs began with Herder

Now I anticipate objections: such sentimentalized figures as "the itinerant tinker" belong in poems and children's books but not in a scholarly analysis of Kollár's ideas; Kollár was a romantic and a dreamer, he idealized the Slavs, and such idealization has done the Slavs a disservice; only the search for truth can serve a useful purpose.

True. Kollár idealized the Slavs, there is considerable unreality, fantasy, and plain untruth in his ideas, and there is no question that there was a harmful side to his activity. But does such an admission and condemnation exhaust the matter? No, certainly not.

Professor Sobyestiansky reproaches Kollár directly—and indirectly attacks most of the Slavicists from Šafařík to the present day —for having written about the Slavs sentimentally and poetically rather than truthfully and realistically.

I agree with Sobyestiansky, to some extent and from a particular viewpoint. In recent times, the crucial issue concerned with Slavic character was the dispute about the forged manuscripts. I have already made some comments in this regard, but only incidentally and without going into detail, and I therefore wish to go into the matter somewhat more deeply at this point, particularly in connection with Kollár's work.

Sobyestiansky analyzed the position of Herder, Surowiecki, Karamzin, Šafařík, he examined the post-Šafařík criticism of Slavic historical literature, he studied the old sources dealing with the character of the ancient Slavs, and finally he surveyed the contemporary works on the legal practices of our ancient Slavic ancestors. On the basis of all these studies Sobyestiansky came to the following conclusions.

The doctrine of the peaceful character of the ancient Slavs arose from an a priori conviction, rather than from critical examination of sources. The humanist philosophy of Herder and the democratic ideas of Rousseau were especially influential in forming an idealized picture of our ancestors. These preconceptions led Slavicists to the assertion that the Slavs were peaceful farmers occupying themselves with agriculture and music. As a consequence of this formulation, they had to admit that the Slavs were incapable of military activity and that they willingly subjected themselves to all foreign invaders. Furthermore, the Slavicists of this Romantic school had to acknowledge that the Slavs learned the military arts from the Huns, Avars, and especially the Germans. Finally, it had to be conceded that the Slavs were incapable of forming and maintaining a stable state: loving freedom above all else, they tolerated no authority.

However, Sobyestiansky points out, these opinions are false. If the sources are examined without prejudice, the antithesis between Slav and Teuton fades away, and this much becomes obvious: the ancient history of the Slavs parallels the history of all nations evolving out of a primitive stage of society. History knows no golden age when nations lived in peace, harmony and total freedom. Nor did the ancient Slavs enjoy a "social idyll"; after all, it would be absurd to suppose that the Slavs initially lived a glorious, noble existence to turn wild and cruel at a subsequent stage of development. A dispassionate analysis of old documents demonstrates that the old Slavs were a bellicose, enterprising, and cruel nation, and all of their recorded existence is in accord with these national traits. Refinement of moral awareness only began with the great cultural upheaval caused by Christianization. Those Slavic tribes that clung to paganism the longest were also the ones that maintained their original primitive character. This is the reason—rather than proximity to barbaric nations—why the Baltic Slavs long continued to exhibit ferocity, slavery, polygamy, and the killing of children and the aged, as well as human sacrifice.

Sobyestiansky ascribes the idealization of Slavs mainly to political motivation, particularly of a nationalistic kind.

According to Sobyestiansky, the distorted views on the Slavs stemmed from the late eighteenth century, especially from the writings of Herder; subsequently they were taken over by men such as Surowiecki, Šafařík, and Kollár. Because of the prestige attached to these names, the idealized view still prevails. From the most ancient times all the way to Herder, the Slavs were commonly described as brave, pugnacious, cruel, and savage. Sobyestiansky particularly cites the writings of the Lusatian author Anton from the year 1783, in which the older and correct view was given extensive treatment. In Russia, it was Karamzin who still held the older, more correct estimate of Slavic character.

Methodological rules that the author finds useful in studying and evaluating nations, especially Slavic nations

This is the substance of the opinions of our Russian critic. I do not wish to embark on an analysis of Sobyestiansky's whole book. However, I must point out where he is right and where wrong. Furthermore, the question of Slavic character will return over and over again, so we may as well come to grips with it right here.

I accept Sobyestiansky's valid critcism that numerous Slavic authors—and non-Slavic as well—are guided by nationalistic rather than scholarly motives. I shall therefore submit a concise summary of the criteria I use in judging the character of a nation, whether Slavic or any other.

General Principles

1. It is possible to evaluate nations—including one's own—quite objectively, and there is no necessity for idealization. For example, I am aware of the shortcomings of the Slovaks, yet the Slovaks are no less close to me as a result. I cannot understand why a perception of reality should mar the natural affection toward one's own people, language, and nation. I do not believe in chosen peoples. There is no need for degrading other nations in order to make

one's own excel. I recognize the shortcomings of other nations as well, but these do not sting as much as my own faults or those of my own people. I freely acknowledge the virtues of other peoples, but these in no way diminish the feelings for my own. I consider it a moral duty to speak about all nations sincerely and openly; nationalistic superpatriotism stands in the way of progress.

2. I am becoming increasingly convinced that conclusions regarding national character are generally incorrect or at the very least, superficial. People generally judged others only from what they can see—food, drink, clothes. Superficial, physical characteristics have a strong influence on judgment of character; it is of course extremely difficult to learn about the soul of a man or a people. This is why I take any conclusions regarding national character with extreme caution and distrust, and I myself am most hesitant to make similar pronouncements. It is not enough to observe certain isolated social arrangements, individual spiritual or physical characteristics. I would not dare to express generalized praise or condemnation.

3. As in looking at a man, in looking at a nation I am mainly concerned with soul and spirit. I do not regard a language as holy in itself, but as a means of serving the spirit for good or evil. Naturally, the mother tongue is the most intimate means of expression and consequently the most effective. In disputes among nations I am primarily concerned with the spiritual aspect of the struggle; ideas, feelings, moral goals are decisive. To deprive a people of their language is a form of barbarism and political materialism. At the same time, I believe that matter can only be combatted by spirit; that is why I have long ago resigned from the fold of fetishistic wordmongers and nationalistic fanatics. Morality and humanism must be the goals of every individual and every nation. No nation has a right to its own special set of ethics.

Specific Principles

4. We are not satisfied with a study of abstract Slavism—we study Czechs, Poles, Russians, Serbs. We reject hasty generalizations. Only those characteristics which all Slavs share in equal measure are to be considered Slavic.

5. By studying the contemporary Slavs, we will gain a better

understanding of the ancient Slavs. A comparative study of the living Slavs is a far more reliable method than a shaky historicism, which has special affinity for the darkest and most inaccessible parts of our distant past. Illumine the past with the light of the present; the reverse process is an illusion.

6. Let us stop regarding political and military events as the sum total of the life of nations. A psychological and historical analysis of the Bohemian Brethren, of their teachings and church organization, or an analysis of the Russian *Domostroy* will tell us more about the character of the Slavs than the reports of a sixth-century Byzantine emperor. A comparative study of Goethe's *Faust* and Dostoevsky's *Brothers Karamazov* will speak more articulately about the German and Russian character than dozens of pronouncements by demagogues on both sides—notwithstanding the place of honor that demagoguery is enjoying these days.

7. Analogy with other nations is always a good guide, since people living in similar times under similar circumstances are far more akin to each other than would appear at first glance. And in spite of the fact that humanity is gradually evolving, basic human nature has not changed to any appreciable extent.

8. Nature and general environment exert a continual strong influence on individuals as well as on nations. A study of such an influence would solve many questions that are considered intrinsically national. Do not ascribe to the soul what you find on the body —or perhaps only on the overcoat.

9. More and more, I am coming to the conclusion that the people most akin to the Slavs in temperament are the Germans. Of course, this can be gathered from any scholarly book on ethnography, but the important thing is to make this discovery on one's own, from life and from literature, and to act accordingly. One consequence that follows from this observation is my conviction that German influences did not have nearly as harmful an effect on the Czech character as many Slavophiles believe. In any case, the creation of artificial distinctions between nations is ineffectual both from a political and nationalistic viewpoint. Political evolution is guided by realities, not fictions.

Harmful influences of a foreign nature can best be combatted by the strength of one's own spirit. This goes on unconsciously. However, as soon as people become aware of this process and start to think about it, there is no other alternative but to embark upon the most painstaking and conscientious self-analysis and examination of foreign influences and thus to replace unconscious, instinctive behavior by deliberate, purposeful action.

Are the Slavs peace-loving? / The meaning of such a trait / The judgment of Leroy-Beaulieu regarding the Russians / Slavic attitudes toward violence / Žižka and the Brethren

Now, I hope, we can come to an understanding with Professor Sobyestiansky. First of all then, the main question: are the Slavs different from the Germans, Latins, and other peoples by an inherent humaneness that has manifested itself historically in politics and warfare?

My answer is: Yes! The Slavs do indeed differ by virtue of this quality; however, it is necessary to define it, to determine its limits. Does this mean that the Slav was not a brave soldier? Sobyestiansky correctly showed that the Slavs considered themselves brave and that this opinion was always shared by outside observers.

Does this mean that the Slavs were not coarse, raw, or cruel? No. Some natures may be both mild and cruel; such extremes often coexist. It seems to me that this duality is especially typical of the Russians, as their greatest artists and writers repeatedly confirm by analyzing the character of their people. I observe this in Mitya Karamazov, in Repin's *Ivan the Terrible*, I sense it in living persons. Even non-Slavic observers have remarked on this aspect of the Russian character. I could refer to a long series of literary and other statements, including those of Leroy-Beaulieu. I wish to cite at least a few sentences from this author. Leroy-Beaulieu places far too great an emphasis on Russian climate, claiming that climatic extremes of the weather are responsible for the Russian temperament. I doubt that climate has anything like the significance ascribed to it, but here we are not concerned with how the Russian character came into being but only with its present nature. Leroy-Beaulieu sees in the Russian character great passivity, patience, and resignation verging on fatalism. "The Russian soldier is the most unyielding in Europe. In this respect he can be compared only to his old foe, the Turk. Both have a capacity to suffer with a stoicism that is quite foreign to the nations of Western

Europe. And yet by nature the Russian people are the least war-like of the peoples of Europe. At no period of history did the Russians behave aggressively. Peace-loving by nature, the Russian looks upon war only as a scourge to which he submits in his obedience to God and to the Czar."

Further, Leroy-Beaulieu points out the peculiar combination of hardness and cordiality, sensitiveness and kind-heartedness. In war the Russian soldier is pitiless, yet immediately after the battle he is naïvely good-hearted and magnanimous. He is cruel yet gentle. The Russian is not steadfast, especially when success seems doubtful. The Russian mind is practical and positive, it is not comfortable with abstractions, it does not care for metaphysical speculation, it does not enjoy penetrating to the heart of things. Rather, it prefers to occupy itself with natural and social sciences. "There are few nations so completely devoid of sentimentality and at the same time so proud of this lack." Fondness for practical common sense at times reaches the point of brutality; it was a Russian who proclaimed that a pair of shoes is more useful than Pushkin. The Russian is a realist, a naturalist. The Russian soul is melancholy—Herzen called great Russian folk songs "sounding tears." This melancholy gives birth to mysticism, which tends to obscure the basic Russian realistic attitude to life; this is evident in such writers as Gogol and Dostoevsky. Russian melancholy is combined with a devotion and piety that is extraordinary. The Russian muzhik has amazing calmness and poise, and even when drunk he is quiet and peaceable.

Here we find everything that Kollár, Herder, and others have told us about the character of the Slavs. We would reach a similar conclusion through an analysis of characters out of Tolstoy, Dostoevsky, Garshin, Turgenev, as well as through the philosophic ideas of Kireyevsky, Kollár, and Šafařík. After all, the humanist idea has taken firm root in all these Slavic thinkers. This fact must signify at least as much as the testimony of Emperor Mauritius, the historian Procopius, and other ancient gentlemen whom Stritter and his fellow scholars have dug up from old documents. An analysis of non-Slavic authors who have devoted themselves to Slavic studies also supports the conclusions presented above.

This, then, is the sense in which the Russians are peaceable and thus humane. A similar statement can be made about the Poles and the Czechs. Our ferocious Hussites and Taborites were balanced by the Bohemian Brethren—another example of the Slavic character.

However, it is difficult to say whether peaceableness is necessarily a quality superior to Germanic fierceness. Both traits have their good and bad sides. At issue is neither a raw and unmitigated bloodthirstiness nor an idealistic pacifism entirely free of undesirable components. I have already expressed doubts as to whether Kollár's humanist ideal could be realized in the face of total Slavic passivity.

Another question presses to the fore—namely, whether we Slavs prefer our own qualities or those of other peoples, especially when we are not convinced of our own superiority. In any case, these matters are at bottom rather simple and present no practical obstacles; only scholars like to make these questions seem complicated.

Czechs and Germans / Instructive tale of the death of cats

I am of course aware that my references to Leroy-Beaulieu were concerned with contemporary Russia rather than the ancient Slavs. To some extent, however, the relationship between Russians and Germanic peoples was quite similar centuries ago to what it is today.

But let us leave the Russians aside for the moment. What is the significant difference between the Germans and ourselves?

In my Slavic studies I have naturally devoted considerable time to a consideration of this question and to the formulation of my views. I had found this matter quite puzzling until one day I happened to discuss it with a German friend. He told me a true story; although trivial, it is eloquent in analyzing the differing national character of Czech and German. The anecdote is innocent, it concerns the killing—of cats. As the reader will see, the death of a few cats occasioned more analysis and introspection than many a military expedition of the fifth century about which whole tomes have been written by historians.

In the northeastern part of our territory a Czech recently bought an estate. One of the farms on it was located in a Czech village and its steward was a Czech, while the other piece of property was in a German-speaking village and had a German manager. My friend, who is a clergyman in the region, had good occasion to follow the story.

The new Czech owner hated cats. It was a definite idiosyncracy, and he was incensed to find that the steward kept a goodly number of these animals on the property, primarily to keep away mice.

My friend related that the owner was getting increasingly more nervous about the cats, but to his surprise no order was given that the animals were to be removed. With each succeeding visit to his estate, the owner always managed to make some derogatory remarks about the cats—but he gave no explicit direction about them.

Finally, one day he pointedly asked his steward "whether the cats were still around." The Czech manager, who had been getting increasingly uneasy by the owner's hints, now consulted his wife. She advised him to get rid of the animals, and he did accordingly. The owner seemed pleased that the hated creatures had vanished, but he said nothing.

On the German side, the cats still remained in full force, until one day the owner said: "Your colleague, Mr. Vávra, has gotten rid of all the cats." Steward Schmidt thereupon inquired whether the gentleman wanted the cats removed from the German estate as well. The owner nodded, and shortly both estates were entirely free of cats.

After a time, however, the yards were overrun with mice. The owner came to realize that his urban prejudices would have to be subordinated to the realities of country life, if the grain was not to be entirely eaten up by mice.

And now the story unfolds in reverse. The owner began to drop hints about the usefulness of cats, Vávra consulted his wife and upon her advice replenished the cats in the yard. The owner praised Vávra for his perspicacity. Shortly thereafter, Schmidt asked the owner: "Do you wish me to buy some cats again?" "It may not be a bad idea," replied the owner, and soon cats were fully rehabilitated on the German side of the border as well.

You see, explained my German friend, there you have the two types: the Slav, the German. A German owner would have simply given the necessary orders, expecting them to be obeyed. The

Czech owner does not command directly, but lets his subordinates guess his wishes. The German steward refuses to guess, but in a manly and open manner asks the owner. In this way, a direct order must be given and is obeyed.

This example, continued my clerical friend, gave me much to think about. I asked myself which of the two stewards I liked better. I must say I prefer the Czechs, both the owner and the steward, because they seem to have more sensitivity, more sympathy. Of course, the German directness is admirable, but it has less of a human quality.

And how do you think the Czech owner himself felt about it, I asked my friend. It seems he was more impressed by the German steward, he replied.

This is my anecdote about cats. I can assure you that it has taught me more about Czech and German character than many a learned dissertation. I have repeatedly analyzed this story for myself; in particular, the words about German "directness" stuck in my mind. I recalled that the Slavs—and especially the Czechs— are commonly reproached for a tendency to deviousness and lying. I recalled that we Slavs often level the same accusation at ourselves; Dostoevsky, for example, condemned Russian untruthfulness. And I tried to determine whether the softness and timidity of our Czech landowner was not the timidity of a man afraid to look people in the eye, in other words the timidity of an insincere man. But then again, I pondered, why do the Russians have two expressions for the word "to lie"? Does not that imply that there are two kinds of untruth? And could not our Czech "falseness" derive to some extent from our lack of independence, so that at bottom we are not really devious—but merely "indirect," as my friend expressed it? Germans and other non-Slavic people do not understand this "indirectness." Then again, does not this attitude easily slide into real, ugly insincerity? On the other hand, said the Czech advocate in my brain, does not German directness too often degenerate into arrogance and coarseness?

I admitted my uncertainties to my friend. It seemed that he did not sympathize with my perturbation. By return mail I received his answer: "Just compare the message preached by Czech reformers with that of the German ones—Hus and Luther, for example—and you will recognize echoes of Vávra and Schmidt. Can't you see that your Czech mildness required the backbone of a Wycliffe or a Luther?"

The letter cheered me and saddened me at the same time. Was Luther really essential to make our reformation a success?

I know that the Byzantine emperors who had written so much about Slavic character must be turning in their graves. But granted that we are mild-mannered, perhaps a certain amount of self-suggestion might be all we need to carry out our firm and laudable intentions. There is an anecdote about some Slavic peasants who needed a road and were quite ready and willing to build it themselves. However, in order to gather sufficient momentum to get the job underway, they petitioned a government office to *order* them to begin at once.

A similar story concerns two Russian soldiers examining an enemy fortress. First soldier: "Can we storm it?" Second soldier, after expert scrutiny: "No. Impossible." "But suppose they order us to take it." "Well, then we'll do it, naturally."

And so the soft, peaceable muzhik becomes an excellent soldier, a mild person turns unbelievably brave. Yes, all that is needed is to issue orders to ourselves.

Sobyestiansky's inaccurate interpretation of old sources and of Herder's philosophy

I beg the reader's pardon for having digressed from the tone of a serious critical work, although our consideration of national character was not really too far from our central subject. In any case, we shall now return to the conclusions of Professor Sobyestiansky.

As mentioned earlier, Sobyestiansky cites the historian Anton as having formulated a more correct concept of the Slavs than did Herder. In Anton's writings [*Erste Linien eines Versuches...*, 1783], Sobyestiansky sees a confirmation of the views prevalent earlier than Herder, namely that the Slavs were brave, warlike, savage, and cruel, like many other nations. Let us assume that Anton is correct. He has certainly conducted extensive research into this question, drawing not only on ancient authorities but utilizing his knowledge of Slavic languages and making observations among living Slavs.

I have read Anton's work thoroughly, but my impression is considerably different from that of Sobyestiansky. Contrary to Sobyestiansky's assertion Anton does not portray the Slavs as warlike, cruel, or savage. It is true that Anton describes the Slavs as a military people, but he presents their warlike qualities as being significantly different from those of the Germans. When the belligerent nature of the Slavs is placed in the context of all the other Slavic traits discussed by Anton, the distinction between the Germans and Slavs becomes quite clear.

Anton makes a specific differentiation between Slavs and Germans in several respects. On the basis of the oldest sources, the major distinction between the two peoples supposedly derives from the early preference that the Slavs have shown for agriculture. Consequently, it is concluded that the Slavs were less warlike than the Germans, who were actually ashamed of any agricultural labor. In his work on the Slavs, Anton makes no particular mention of this matter, and therefore the point has likewise eluded Sobyestiansky. However, Anton has also written a history of the ancient Germans, using the same method and approach as in his work on the Slavs. This companion volume [*Geschichte der Teutschen Nazion*, 1793] throws into sharp relief many matters that would be unclear if we limited ourselves to Anton's work on the Slavs.

For example, in the history of the Germans we read that every nation—including the Slavs—evolved from a savage state to a barbaric state and finally to that of civilization. The Germans, when they came in contact with the Romans, were no longer savages. Among striking Germanic traits were belligerence and love of freedom. Bravery was highly valued while hard labor was treated with contempt; the Germans preferred to shed blood rather than to earn their bread in the sweat of their brow.

In his chapter on war, Anton describes Germanic bravery entirely differently from the way he treated the corresponding quality among the Slavs. The reader gets the impression that Anton's eyes must have glistened as he enthusiastically describes the terror of the German attack, the military efficiency with which conquered peoples were organized and enslaved. When the German was not making war, he hunted. He considered that it was ignoble to secure food and shelter through heavy labor, and he relegated slaves to perform these tasks.

Anton did not diminish the difference between German and Slav as far as belligerence is concerned. On the contrary, he confirmed that such a difference in fundamental attitude existed. I repeat, nevertheless, that it is wrong to idealize the past in a Rousseau-like manner—in this Sobyestiansky is quite correct. Our ancestors were certainly crude, coarse and cruel, but their temperament was not as aggressive as was the German.

Similarly, Sobyestiansky is not sufficiently accurate in explaining Herder's attitude to the Slavs. As we noted earlier, Herder did not maintain that the Slavs lacked courage. He merely stated that the Slavs loved peace, refused to organize themselves permanently on a military footing, and as a consequence were defeated by the more bellicose Germans. Herder pointed out that the Slavs did not strive for conquest but were farmers and tradesmen. Once subjugated, they became devious and cruel and developed a lazy, slavish mentality. I admit, however, that even Herder conceived of the olden times—in particular as far as the Slavs were concerned —in far too idyllic terms. In this he showed himself to be a pupil of Rousseau. As far as the supposed Slavic fondness for agriculture is concerned, Herder may have been influenced by contemporary physiocratic ideas, which have also affected Rousseau. In funda-mental matters, however, Herder correctly summarized and in-terpreted information about the Slavs provided by a variety of old and recent sources.

Sobyestiansky is wrong in maintaining that Herder idealized the Slavs. And even if he did, he displayed the same attitude toward the Germans. We only have to read the chapter on the German people in Herder's *Ideen zur Philosophie der Geschichte der Menschheit* to see that this is true. He described the Germans in a way similar to Anton, he portrayed them as heroes who eschewed manual labor. According to Herder, this has remained a German characteristic down to modern times. Herder noted that even closely related tribes had many an occasion to feel the keenness of the German sword and so did the "unfortunate Slavs, Prussians, Kurs, Letts, and Estonians." The Germans also repelled the wild

Huas, Hungarians, Mongols, and Turks. "Thus, it was the Germans who conquered the greater part of Europe, cultivated it, and protected it from outside incursions. Otherwise, European development as we know it could not have taken place. The stature of Germans among other nations, their military prowess, and ethnic qualities became the foundations (*Grundfesten*) of European culture, freedom, and security. History, that uncorruptible witness, also reports the contribution that German political developments made to the gradual progress of European civilization."

Herder thus sees in the special military aptitude of the Germans a major cause of European cultural evolution. The Slavs were not as warlike, and therefore they succumbed to the Germans. However, as we read previously, Herder believed that a nonmilitary epoch has not yet arisen and the peaceable Slavs will finally come into their own.

We have already discussed the faith in the future of humanism as expressed by Herder and a number of other thinkers. Here we are merely recalling certain aspects of Herder's thought in order to point out the erroneous interpretations made by Sobyestiansky. Herder never maintained that only the Slavs would bring about the humanization of mankind; that was Kollár's idea. Herder anticipated a nonmilitary European federation in which all nations would participate to realize the principle of humaneness. For Herder, militarism was only a temporary expedient for humanization, just as it was for modern sociologists such as Comte and Spencer.

The extent of Kollár's uncritical idealization of Slavs / Kollár's opinions regarding the peaceableness of Slavs do not merely stem from Herder / Kollár's own conception of Slavic gentleness

Let us examine Kollár's opinion of the Slavs. Sobyestiansky attacked Kollár indirectly—and Šafařík directly—for idealizing the ancient and contemporary Slavs and for describing their character poetically and sentimentally.

It is true that Kollár was guilty of uncritical idealization. However, his distortion did not derive from ascribing undue humaneness and mildness to the Slavs but from painting their foes in excessively dark colors. In many respects, he was unfair to our adversaries. We have already discussed this earlier. On the other hand, for the sake of accuracy we must also recall the deplorable manner in which German, Hungarian, and other foreign authors write about the Slavs—and I am thinking of authors of the first rank. I am quite well acquainted with this literature, and I can say dispassionately that even from this point of view a certain German arrogance and aggressiveness comes to the fore. For example, if Hegel so one-sidedly ascribed absolute primacy to his nation, why be surprised that Kollár did the same for his own people? I admitted that here and there Kollár expressed more animosity toward our national opponents than suited a philosopher. On the other hand, the same Kollár has also wholeheartedly acknowledged German benevolence, including that of Herder.

Kollár's idealized view of the Slavs is also distorted by his seizing upon relatively minor faults while overlooking our major failings. He has repeatedly taken us to task for a lack of enlightenment. In reality, he should have searched far deeper, and he should have placed more blame for our decline on our own failings than on the malice and envy of our enemies. His lamentation and reproaches regarding the fate of the Polabian Slavs are especially ill-founded; Germans as well as several other peoples have lost territory to Russian expansion.

We have objectively admitted these and other errors and shortcomings of Kollár. But even an inspired poet would find it difficult to write a new *Slávy dcera* nowadays, especially if he had to follow my precepts. The old romanticism is dying out.

Kollár's uncritical attitude toward the Slavs does not only stem from patriotic fervor but it reflects a deficient scholarly method. This, too, has already been touched on. We must especially emphasize that Kollár erroneously ascribed common characteristics to all the Slavs, whereas in reality there are considerable differences between individual Slavic peoples. With respect to bellicosity, for example, Polish bravery surely differs from Montenegrin ferocity or Russian fortitude. A detailed psychological and sociological analysis would uncover a spectrum of quantitative and qualitative shadings. As we pointed out earlier, Kollár unconsciously identified Slovak qualities with Slavic ones.

Nor does Kollár adequately differentiate between ancient and contemporary Slavs. External conditions of life were quite varied in ancient times, and this in itself is responsible for a differentiation of qualities, even though perhaps not of a basic kind.

Kollár was, of course, equally inexact in portraying the traits of the Germans. As a result of all these errors Kollár established a difference between Germans and Slavs which is so absolute as to belie his basic philosophical tenet of common humanity. Kollár was not capable of harmoniously reconciling his national and humanistic ideals.

As Sobyestiansky observed, the idealization of Slavs does not only stem from Herder but from the Slavs themselves; we Czechs and Slovaks have been especially guilty in this respect. Sobyestiansky's demand for a more objective, critical attitude is quite justified. But in fairness to our "idealists" I have to mention one more consideration. Kollár, as we have seen, wavered between a Slavic reciprocity either literary or national-political. Kollár was by no means blind to the complexities involved in the question of Slavic mildness. In answer to an accusation of excessive Slavic malleability, he stated: "The Slavs have sufficient strength and energy. With courage and virility, they have secured dominance over one tenth of the globe, they have protected their territory during the furious storms of centuries and have resisted violent onslaughts of numerous foes. It is true that the Slavs never strove for world domination, they never made it a practice to shed blood and to subjugate other nations. They honored liberty, even the liberty of their foes, they loved freedom, and they preferred peace to war."

We may thus summarize our answer to Professor Sobyestiansky this way: Kollár was guilty of excessive idealization of the Slavs, but Sobyestiansky exaggerated the importance of this failing and erred in analyzing its causes.

 CHAPTER 4

Completion of the
Czech National Renascence

*Havlíček and his mission / His continuous struggle
against spiritual reaction; religious reform his life's ideal /
Havlíček as a realistic, modern, progressive person / Havlíček
as critic revolutionized literature*

During the mournful period of reaction, Havlíček stood on guard, continuing his beneficent literary and political work.

We have no more magnificent figure in our modern era, and I do not know whether I shall be able, in this brief space, to do justice to Havlíček's providential significance for our nation. I shall attempt to do so.

During the repressive period of reaction, when Havlíček became our national leader, the question of tactics assumed crucial importance. I see Havlíček's greatness in the fact that he knew his goal more clearly than anyone else and that he continued to strive for that goal with steadfast firmness before the revolution, during the revolution, and after the revolution; Havlíček had virile perseverance, and knowing the means to be employed he refused to be swayed by anything—not even by the general excitement—and he

From Tomáš G. Masaryk, *Česká otázka: Snahy a tužby národního obrození* (Prague, 1969), Chapter III.

[76]

veered neither too far to the left nor to the right. In this regard, Havlíček will continue to serve as our teacher for a long time to come. In spite of his level-headed composure, Havlíček did not escape persecution and political martyrdom. Tyranny has good reason to be more worried by steady, determined opposition than by momentary, passionate flare-ups of resistance. Falsehood is most afraid of truth, and Havlíček was a genuine man—this is the best way to describe his indefatigable efforts, his persistent activity logically directed at a predetermined goal.

Havlíček dedicated his entire life to reviving and strengthening our national awareness and our language. His faith in our cause was demonstrated not only by his inspired speeches but by his insistence upon writing exclusively in Czech at a time when our best thinkers were still using German. In spite of his cosmopolitan outlook and careful attention to world events he was content with his own native land.

His slogan "Czech, not Slav" had a deep significance for Havlíček, not because he rejected Slavic sentiments and allegiance, but because he was firmly convinced that only a genuine Czech, a Czech through and through, could be a true Slav. And Havlíček was a pure Czech; among our writers and public figures he was a model of the national sense of identity.

Having grasped the spirit of Czech history, Havlíček was an authentic free thinker. He based all of his political activity on his dedication to the principle of free thought. He told us himself that the forces of reaction had discovered this source of his strength and that he was subjected to merciless attack precisely because he was fundamentally a defender of the liberty of thought and feeling. Havlíček was free of that stultifying and indifferent rationalism that paralyzed so many of our patriots. Havlíček never wrote a single line that was not consistent with the principles of inner freedom—this was the reason for his effectiveness in combatting reaction, as well as the reason for his persecution. In other words, the enmity he incurred at home and in Vienna could not be attributed to his political opinions but to the authenticity of his philosophical convictions and his unswerving opposition to spiritual obscurantism.

In 1848–49, as well as in subsequent years, he published a thorough critique of clerical and religious matters; he disclosed the shortcomings of clerical administration and demanded reform. His *Epištoly Kutnohorské (Epistles from Kutná Hora)* is but one of the fruits of this activity. Of course, as a politician and journalist he did not attempt profound philosophic or theologic analysis. However, all of his articles make it evident that he was personally concerned with such questions and devoted time and energy to them. This was clearly evident when he published the last testament of Bolzano, and in this connection commented in a modest, yet all the more moving, way on the philosopher's opinions regarding the ultimate questions of life. Even some of Havlíček's admirers prefer to overlook this side of his activity—our vulgar liberalism fears the ultimate questions of life as the devil fears holy water. But anyone who fails to understand this facet of Havlíček fails to grasp not only Havlíček's mind but the entire meaning of Czech history and Czech spirit. It was no accident that Havlíček was drawn toward the priesthood, nor was it an accident that he overcame his attraction and lived the tortured life of a soul torn by the struggle between an old faith and a new one.

Even Havlíček's literary form was consistent with his aspirations. His realistic genuineness and purity of conviction expressed themselves in a simple popular style and found a language that was truly Czech, alive, even though it irritated grammarians and linguistic purists. As a Czech and a Slav, Havlíček was a realist in the same sense as the greatest Russian authors. If Palacký was the father of the nation, Havlíček was the nation's popular son.

Havlíček derived his most powerful influence from his dual role as journalist and man of letters. The period required this type of literary form, and Havlíček filled the need. Havlíček provides an unsurpassed model of a Czech journalist and writer. He demonstrated that even routine, every-day journalistic work can and must present a coherent political opinion and world view. He showed that every written line can and must arise out of a conviction that had been formed through continual reflection upon the demands of social and private life. This is why Havlíček's articles—individually and collectively—present a realistic, logical system of opinions that have not only practical political significance but a theoretical and philosophical foundation as well.

Finally, this brief characterization must include one additional basic quality of Havlíček's mind: his emphasis upon immediate reality. Unlike Kollár, Šafařík, and even Palacký, Havlíček was not addicted to historicism; he examined everything directly in the light of the present. By analyzing the present, he discovered historical processes; he was not detached from life like so many of those who had never succeeded in emancipating themselves from a narrow scholastic outlook. Havlíček was a man who lived entirely in the present; in fact, he was a man of the future, a truly modern and progressive person.

This is the reason for Havlíček's success as critic and political analyst. He lived in the present, and turning his eyes toward the future, he saw our goals and shortcomings in clear relief. The logical starting-point for Havlíček was therefore criticism of the present; he was our first truly critical spirit after Dobrovský. This activity was necessary in order to remove the sham that had marked our intellectual life of the time. His article on Russia fell like a thunderbolt on the heads of pseudopatriots and Slavophiles. His attack on Tyl revealed at a single stroke the moral decay behind our vulgar chauvinism. In short, Havlíček revolutionized our spirit and our literary life, and he thus fulfilled the most pressing need of the time.

Havlíček and Palacký agree on demand for Austrian federation /
Havlíček supported natural right based on Rousseau's social
contract

As far as a political program is concerned, Havlíček basically agreed with Palacký. He dedicated his *Duch národních novin* (*Spirit of the Nation's Newspaper*) to Palacký. He differed from Palacký not so much in basic concepts as in his political methods; but of course, in politics differences in means can be extremely significant.

Above all, Havlíček supported Palacký in demanding an Austrian federation. His thoughts on this matter, as well as his fundamental concept of the state, are expressed in an article entitled "Our Task," published in *Národní noviny* of 23 May 1849:

We cannot but oppose a *government* that has not fulfilled its purposes. However, let us hold fast to *Austria*, which is the guarantor of our existence. Sooner or later, Austria must undertake the task assigned to it by Providence, namely to become a central European union of free nations. Let us keep this goal constantly before our eyes, and let us continue to work for it with fortitude and perseverance. Let us sway neither to the left nor to the right, let us maintain continuous and unified opposition to the government, an opposition conducted strictly within the limits of the law, making up with spiritual force for the lack of our material resources. In all of our striving let us always be sustained by genuine democracy, which had from the very beginning constituted the life and soul of our national endeavor. This is our task, this is the path toward our salvation.

Of course, like Palacký, Havlíček favored a federation of peoples rather than of national territories. In his well-known article "On Centralization and National Equality in Austria," Palacký divided the Austrian realm into seven national population groups. At Havlíček's request, Palacký published this article in *Národní noviny* (21 December 1849).

Havlíček adhered to this national program even after the years 1848 and 1849. Palacký, on the other hand, ultimately gave up the idea of a federation based on purely national entities as "connected with revolution." He accepted the Eötvös concept of a historico-political individuality [i.e., of the historical right of the kingdoms of Bohemia and Hungary], which reflects the historical realities of any given period and which is essentially antirevolutionary.

Havlíček was more radical in this regard, always answering to natural law. He was thus closer to the ideals of Kollár than Palacký. In his notion of the state Havlíček abided by Rousseau's theory of the social contract and generally agreed with the political philosophy elaborated in France at the end of the eighteenth century.

The democratic movement of 1848 / Havlíček, Palacký, Rieger: "All state power derives from the people"

In accord with the spirit of his time, Havlíček favored democratic principles as the foundations of the state. He did not demand a republic even in the time of the upheaval (of 1848); he correctly saw that a republic in itself does not guarantee freedom. Havlíček did not consider democracy as antithetical to monarchy; rather, he saw the opposite of democracy in aristocracy. He therefore favored an Austrian democratic state.

Palacký also opposed republicanism, as was already evident in his message to Frankfurt. He believed in a democratic program, conceiving of democracy in the sense of strict constitutionalism. But while Havlíček contrasted his concept of democracy with aristocracy, Palacký came to terms with the aristocracy and therefore moved toward a more conservative position. Havlíček stuck to his guns and was supported at the Kremsier constitutional assembly by Rieger.

Palacký and Havlíček on democracy and on the social question / Palacký opposed universal suffrage, Havlíček favored it / The extensive and intensive nature of humanism

Various theories of democracy frequently contain widely differing views and positions; the word "democracy" meant quite different things to Palacký and to Havlíček. As we mentioned earlier, Palacký understood "government of the people" within the context of contemporary constitutionalism. On the other hand, Havlíček already saw democracy in terms of a certain "populism," namely a government in which even the lowest classes of society could exercise their political rights.

In brief, Havlíček was more popularly oriented, more "social-minded" than Palacký. When using common political terminology in alluding to these two men, the fine nuances and distinctions in their respective concepts must be borne in mind.

The difference between the political ideal of Palacký and of Havlíček is most strikingly evident in their respective attitudes to problems now labeled as "social questions."

Behind the attempts to improve the conditions of the workers Palacký saw excessive revolutionary agitation and especially communism; he declared that communism would bring about a barbaric society within a single generation. He recognized the validity of socialism only as long as it employed the theory and practice of early Christianity and of the Bohemian Brethren. Love and benevolence were to eradicate injustice. Palacký advised the workers to present their grievances through calm and legal means, in the confidence that justice would eventually prevail. His main argument against socialism was the natural inequality of human beings. For the same reason, he opposed the universal right to vote. In this regard, he identified himself with the position of the aristocracy and its historic privileges. He spoke about "the proletariat" in terms used by the contemporary bourgeoisie.

In socioeconomic questions, Havlíček also took a liberalistic position. In his article on "The Right to Work" (*Národní noviny*, 17 October 1849), he described the right to work as natural rather than acquired. In accord with Rousseau's contract theory, the right to work preceded the establishment of states; for that reason, the state had no obligation to secure such a right, as revolutionaries and communists demanded. According to Havlíček, the state merely protects work, removes obstacles, etc. Natural right has no specific object; such rights merely guarantee freedom, not property, the latter being the subject of acquired, positive rights.

Havlíček's negative judgment on socialism and communism was still shared by Palacký twenty years later. Havlíček wrote: "It should be self-evident that we do not count such Socialists and Communists as Cabet and Proudhon among liberal and honest persons." He considered communism a form of insanity, and for that reason refused to fear it as dangerous. "Don't worry about those Communists who appropriate pennies, those will be easy to conquer. Rather, fear those Communists who itch to put their hands on millions."

In spite of his antiegalitarian viewpoint, Havlíček supported universal suffrage. The only concession he was willing to make in this regard was to limit the right to vote to persons paying a certain minimum tax, but he wanted to abolish all other class distinctions in political life.

These differences between Havlíček and Palacký are especially relevant at the present time, when the two major parties are so sharply divided on the social question.

Like Kollár, Palacký and Havlíček derived their political philosophy from the concepts of humanism and natural rights of man but differed in the concrete interpretation of these concepts.

The idea of humanism can be conceived both extensively and intensively. The extensive outlook was prominent in the eighteenth century and is still dominant; from the idea of extensive humanism Kollár derived justification for Slavic reciprocity, while Palacký and Havlíček used extensive—or "political"—humanism to legitimize Czech national aspirations.

The noble revolutionary slogan of "liberty, equality, and fraternity" had little actual relevance to the plight of the most underprivileged class of French society, the workers. Similarly, the concepts of humanism and the supreme value of "pure humaneness" did not prevent Palacký from opposing the universal right to vote. "Is it enough to be a man," he asked, "to have a valid voice about the best arrangement of social and national conditions?"

The "populist" concept and its evolution from humanist ideals / The concept of the "folk" as a large mass of the people heretofore disinherited from the common intellectual tradition / The nation and the people as natural cultural units of humanity

Havlíček's most remarkable quality was his "populism." This does not mean that he surpassed his own era in this respect; he was instrumental in preparing a new and more comprehensive movement in our nation. But even Havlíček still understood humanism more politically than socially, in accord with contemporary democratic ideas.

Havlíček's humanism was outstanding, although there is no question that Kollár and his generation paved the way.

Because the concept of humanism is so crucial to our evolution, we will try to provide a brief historical explanation; of course, this question really deserves a special, detailed treatment.

We have seen earlier how the idea of nationality evolved out of humanist theory. Herder was the first apostle of the modern nationalist principle. However, Herder did not conceive of a nation only in ethical terms but took into account its specific cultural unity and creative power. These ideas, too, derived from humanist ideals. Humanism is expressed by the various natural qualities of individual peoples and languages, and every nation is a specific organ of humanity.

In older times the concept of nation was understood only in a political sense. The nation consisted of classes that were politically active and possessed specific rights; the mass of the people had neither political nor cultural rights and was excluded from the intellectual activity of society. Now, since the end of the eighteenth century, the people have been demanding their share in the common intellectual effort and have been playing an increasing cultural role. From a political viewpoint, the mass of the people is still proceeding within the limits of constitutional rules, but it is gradually enlarging the scope of its activity. "The people" are beginning to be regarded as a specific political and cultural entity, contrasted with other existing classes. In our case, the concepts of "nation," "people," and "folk" naturally merge with the concept of Czech-ness and Slav-ness. The word "democratic," too, is being used in the sense of "popular."

Folk culture, as the sum total of everything that simple people feel, think, and create is becoming an object of special study. Formerly, individuals played a decisive role in all aspects of life; now, individuals are disappearing in the mass—in the nation, the people. That is why Herder and so many other outstanding thinkers and poets paid so much attention to folk poetry and literature. The art, the poetry of individuals is rivaled by the art, the poetry of the people. Folk culture is being joined by folk thought and wisdom; attention must now be paid to the political demands of classes hitherto deprived of any rights which actually constitute the vast majority of the population.

The people, in this broad sense of the term, are supplanting individuals; scholastic education and class privilege are being opposed by common sense and by popular rights. In philosophy, the skepticism of Hume is challenged by healthy common sense, a mind that is simple, unschooled, and popular. Academically approved art is opposed by folk art, and privileges of the higher classes are contested by basic rights of the people.

Kollár had learned from his German mentors, especially from Herder, to regard mankind as an organized whole whose evolution serves the great plans of Providence. Herder, Luden, and others had taught Kollár that the agents of these historical, worldwide plans of Providence were not individuals but nations. In the evolution of history, humanity expresses itself by means of particular nations, and at various periods these nations take charge in leading mankind.

In harmony with Herder's teaching as well as with the temper of the times, Kollár collected Slovak folk songs and proclaimed them models for the work of "artificial" poets. In this endeavor Kollár was joined and superceded by men such as Šafařík, Čelakovský, and Erben.

This folk current in literature steadily grew in importance, until in our time it has matured into a systematic science of folklore. However, this brings us to matters that will be discussed later.

Havlíček progressed along this road, enlarging the notion of the nation both politically and socially. We have already emphasized that all of Havlíček's literary activity was of a popular nature and that he earned the right to be termed a popular author in the best sense of the term. All of Havlíček's national activity had this folk character; populism was his most characteristic trait. This attitude also showed his progressiveness. In contrast, Palacký had not yet grasped the significance of populism and nationalism in this intensive sense.

Comparison of the national programs of Havlíček and Palacký

Let us pause for one more moment to clarify the main differences in the attitudes of the two leaders toward our national program.

In spite of overall agreement with respect to the Czech question and in spite of common philosophical foundations, Havlíček's approach differed from Palacký's in a number of significant respects.

First of all, there is the obvious contrast in the social stance of the two men, which has just been elaborated: namely, that Havlíček was considerably more democratic, more down-to-earth than Palacký. Palacký tried to come to terms with the Czech aristocracy, which represented the true political power in the land. This attempt at rapprochement was based on theoretical considerations, as his numerous articles clearly demonstrate, and it was reflected in practical terms as well. Palacký was far more conservative than Havlíček; his attitude to universal suffrage was one clear example.

Thus Havlíček was more progressive, Palacký maintained older socioeconomic principles. This is related to Palacký's propensity toward historicism, and to Havlíček's realistic view of the world. Palacký attempted to reconcile traditional historic rights with natural rights; to Havlíček, such dichotomies were irrelevant. Both in theory and in practice Palacký made concessions to the nobility, often compromising with clerical conservatism and outright reaction. Such compromises were inconsistent with his philosophic convictions.

Havlíček was more nationalistic, Palacký placed greater emphasis on political, constitutional rights. Havlíček wrote only in Czech; Palacký wrote both in Czech and German and delivered his parliamentary addresses in both languages.

Even with regard to the Slavic question the two men had divergent views, although both were committed to the slogan: "Czech, not Slav." The discrepancy in viewpoint was more literary than political. Palacký had no occasion to become acquainted with the Slavic world and Slavic thought, comparable to Havlíček's lengthy sojourn in Russia. For this reason, Palacký viewed Slavicism in a more abstract and restricted sense. But we shall now see that Palacký's trip to Moscow produced a definite change in his outlook.

The emergence of "Old Czech" and "Young Czech" parties / The basis of the Old Czech party / Palacký's appraisal

These differences became crystallized in the course of further evaluation of the two main political parties, the conservative and the freethinking—or, following the usage established by a German journalist—the Old Czechs and the Young Czechs. At first, these differences merely represented an intramural squabble within a single political camp. They were concerned with differing approaches to internal party questions and to cultural and literary problems. Here, we have neither the space nor the inclination to go into some of the more sordid details of these squabbles—for example, the disgraceful affair of the monument to the poet Hálek.

The first teacher of the Old Czech party was Palacký; the first teacher of the Young Czechs was Havlíček. I am convinced that neither of these men would have been pleased by the subsequent development of their spiritual children.

Still under the guidance of Palacký, the Old Czechs carried out certain reactionary policies necessitated by the post-1848 situation. This placed the party at a disadvantage vis-à-vis the more radical movement, which insisted upon the principles established in 1848. Palacký himself abandoned the idea of a national federation in favor of a federation of territories and kingdoms. Rieger, too, gradually abandoned his revolutionary ideals. At the Kremsier assembly Rieger demanded the abolishment of the aristocracy. However, when the parliamentary era was launched in the early 1860s, both Rieger and Palacký accepted the *de facto* leadership of the nobility, which held aloof from the political leaders of 1848. It is true that now and then (e.g., in the Emersdorf agreement) Rieger seemed to return to the ideals of his youth. In essence, however, the Old Czech party accepted the programs and tactics dictated by the forceful political leader Clam-Martinic. After the death of Palacký the leadership of the party was entirely taken over by the nobility, and the representatives of the people were without any real spiritual authority.

This relationship to the aristocracy represents the true, concrete difference between the two parties. Palacký was completely aware of this. In 1864 he explicitly stated that "the question of the relation between the people and the aristocracy has become the apple of discord between us"—that is to say, between the Old Czechs and Young Czechs.

Palacký formulated this diagnosis even more definitely and clearly in his Epilogue in the year 1873. He realized that problems regarding the role of the workers were bound to arise with the related question of universal suffrage. This prediction proved to be correct. Palacký had well perceived his party's growing alienation from more progressive tendencies, with the consequent danger of its decline. The leaders of the aristocracy were unpopularly conservative, socially and philosophically backward, unnational, and consequently also un-Slavic. A narrow-minded caste strove for political hegemony, as in the old days of our history. The Old Czech party, apathetically tolerating this hereditary sin of our aristocracy, consequently degenerated and lost the support of the voting masses. The body and the spirit of the Old Czech party were not in harmonious accord. The party's popular support had no organic way of expressing itself, and the energies of the young artistic and intellectual generation willy-nilly turned to the Young Czechs, even though the actual program enunciated by Palacký was decidedly progressive and liberal-minded. The Old Czechs became nothing but a political organization in the narrowest sense of the word, the party aged and hardened. Kant's categorical imperative, which Palacký had acknowledged as a political credo, turned into tyrannical deadening authoritarianism under the energetic guidance of Clam-Martinic and the nominal leadership of Rieger. The influence emanating from Vienna had only strengthened this internal process, much to the detriment of our nation and of the entire kingdom.

Characterization of the Young Czechs

The orientation of the Young Czech party was more populist or, in its own words, more democratic. It originally received this stamp from Havlíček, and Palacký correctly evaluated its fundamental nature. But just as Palacký would have found it difficult after a few years to recognize the party he had founded, so would Havlíček have felt lost among his former followers.

The popular program of the Young Czechs represented more of a dead remnant of 1848 than a living continuation of the revolutionary heritage. Having served for so long as an opposition party, the Young Czechs increasingly substituted negativism for true criticism and, like all radical parties, came to favor general slogans over concrete, realistic analysis. Just as the Old Czechs rapidly declined after the demise of Palacký, so the Young Czechs failed to find a leader of Havlíček's stature, a man capable of formulating a national political program congruent with the changing needs of the times. For this reason, even outstanding Young Czech deputies admitted confidentially that their program did not substantially differ from that of the rival party. Differences between the two parties narrowed more and more to questions of methods and tactics.

As long as Palacký was alive his authority kept the younger politicians within the bounds of a single camp. After his death this camp split into a number of factions. The mass of the people sympathized with the younger party. Even the intelligentsia was forced to change its allegiance, since intellectual and cultural work is by its very nature progressive.

The liberalism of the Young Czechs was following the development of liberalism elsewhere in Europe, that is to say, it deteriorated. Freethinking became more pale and conventional, turning into run-of-the-mill, vulgar liberalism. There was little humanism in the liberal outlook, for human feelings were pushed into the background by narrow-minded, nationalistic, and economic liberalism with its bourgeois mediocrity.

Our liberalism / Jungmann's tailor who believed in the devil / Jesuit teaching

The question of liberalism and conservatism is a crucial one for our revival and for the entire evolution of our nation. The ultimate choice is this: either a deep, faithful conviction in the existential importance of man—or its rejection. All other questions are subsidiary. Either we commit ourselves to live and to die according to the ideals of Chelčický, Hus, Komenský—or not. Either we want to be true or false; there is no third alternative. A nation that initiated the Reformation and survived the counterreformation cannot afford to be superficial in such matters. And, thank God, our best men lived up to our high tradition.

Our rebirth began with the ideas of the reformation, and these ideas gave us strength. This was clearly evident and pragmatically demonstrated. But we also learned that these reformation ideals were buried under liberalistic indifference. Kollár was not entirely free of this indifference, and the same was unfortunately true of some of his contemporaries.

From the very beginning of our revival, our fathers were given a choice between truth and falsehood, and too many were tempted by tainted fruit.

Jungmann may not have been the father of this questionable liberalism, but he certainly was its main representative. We have already alluded to this matter. Jungmann wholeheartedly believed in the Wieland-Voltaire brand of philosophy, the central slogan of which was Voltaire's pronouncement: "I do not believe in the devil, but I am glad that my tailor does—at least he will not cheat me." The story from Voltaire provided a slogan for all of Jungmann's successors.

Jungmann grounded his philosophy on the spirit of a tailor's religion. To the question of the proper conduct of enlightened priests who were in sympathy with Voltaire, Jungmann gave this advice: "Why give up a rich table for the sake of a lean one? If a good priest gives up his seat, plenty of fools will be found to replace him.... They have no alternative but to keep the truth to themselves and to give the world what the world wants. *Vult mundus decipi, ergo decipiatur.* An old Jesuit rule."

Jungmann's notebooks include an entry suggestion that wise men must occasionally side with the populace in order to propitiate the gods.

Jungmann believed that a man should always be guided by his conscience—except when a higher good is at stake. He cited the example of Socrates, who supposedly believed in a single God yet made sacrifices to many gods. Jungmann declared that "a wise man may honor idols when in the company of savages, with a Mohammedan he may worship in a mosque, with a Christian in a church, if by these means he can teach the truth."

A certain Jesuit—again a Jesuit—declared on the subject of confession that this merely concerns the observance of an ecclesiastic rule, whereas moral goodness is guided by an entirely different set of rules. "Duplicity and hypocrisy," wrote Jungmann, "may thus be condoned to some extent, even when condemned on strictly moral grounds."

This is no longer the philosophy of a tailor believing in the devil but a Smerdyakov. It is the philosophy of a lackey who abjured Christ when threatened by his Asiatic captors, "in order to save his life so that he could ultimately pay with good deeds for his moment of weakness."

Apparently the long and arduous labor of the Jesuits was not wasted in our lands.

Our conservatism / The beginnings of a genuine Catholic literature

To the extent that Catholicism conscientiously opposed this questionable variety of freethinking, one must in all fairness admit the legitimacy of its conservative activity, beginning as early as the Josephine period. Even our foremost freethinking leaders, such as Palacký and Havlíček, opposed the sham aspects of liberalism. But Austrian Catholicism did not have genuine integrity. After defeating the Reformation, particularly our own, Austrian Catholicism reigned unopposed and became a comfortable official creed. Through habit and bureaucratic rigidity it stifled all true progress and freedom.

Bolzano was deposed in 1819; in 1820 the same fate befell Neděle; and reaction overcame Klácel, Smetana, and others. The reactionary governments of Francis I and Bach permitted gambling, dissipation—everything except independent thought.

To the ruling hierarchy any national aspiration smacked of Hussitism. Kamarýt, Ziegler, and others had difficulty in publishing Czech religious songs and sermons. In 1848 the lower clergy led by Náhlovský struggled for church reform, along with Havlíček, even Tomek, and other freethinking persons. However, this movement was easily suppressed. The Austrian clerical hierarchy met in Vienna in June of 1848 and decreed that nationalism was a remnant of paganism and that national differentiation was merely the result of sinfulness and a turning away from God. . . . Sušil was to have been deprived of his professorship for having signed a petition demanding parliamentary elections. To the ecclesiastic leadership, the Czech language was not only a pagan one but a heretic one as well—Archbishop Schwarzenberg refused to proclaim the dogma of infallibility in Bohemia, supposedly fearing Hussite wrath. Actually, however, for countless thousands of Czechs "the nation of Hus" had become but an empty slogan, just as for many others Catholicism and religion had become mere words without real meaning.

It was only considerably later, following the French and German examples, that our Catholicism became organized politically and culturally, forcing comfortable pot-bellied liberalism to take a more realistic view of the world.

Structural changes in Austria / Our shift from passive opposition to a positive political program / Palacký on the relation between world organization and our political independence / Problems of a small nation

We can give here only a brief account of the development of our political constitutionalism and parliamentarianism. Our efforts in 1848 suffered from half-heartedness and feebleness; for the same reasons, we were unable to intervene effectively in the subsequent constitutional and legal reorganization of Austria. We were insufficiently educated politically, and this is still our failing. Our political temperament lacks a firm rational foundation. For centuries, we were governed by an alien power, and now we have ability neither to lead nor to obey.

The October decree brought Palacký into the political arena, and the Polish uprising gave our young parliamentarianism some needed ferment. These conditions inspired Palacký's *Idea státu rakouského* (*The Idea of the Austrian State*, 1865). In the subsequent year, 1866, the process that had begun in 1806 reached its culmination: through its second unsuccessful war, Austria was finally forced to turn inward upon its own problems and to abandon the grandiose hereditary policy of global Catholicism. For many years this had been but an empty gesture in any case.

In this time of need Vienna adopted a set of purely mechanical solutions, giving rise to a Viennese centralism paralleled by a Budapest centralism. In short, dualism. In the meantime, our politicians were busy making speeches in Russia. In the year 1870, the process that had begun in 1806 reached maturity in another sense as well: Protestant Prussia founded the German Empire.

We found ourselves relatively powerless in the face of these developments, and to a considerable extent we must accept the blame for our own impotence. A successful political program must be based on coherent political theory. A successful parliamentary action demands the political awareness of large masses of people, and this situation was lacking in our lands. True, in Palacký and Havlíček we possessed sound political theoreticians. But Havlíček soon left us. Furthermore, the teaching of both men was too new, and it could not be expected that in the course of a few years it would become incorporated into the brain and sinew of the nation. The continual shifts and alterations that Palacký made in his program were also a significant handicap.

Parliamentarianism was alien to us and we found it difficult to make proper use of it. It is true that other nations faced similar problems, especially the Germans and Hungarians. But the German bureaucracy successfully neutralized the effects of parliamentarism, while the Hungarians enjoyed considerable autonomy as well as the benefits achieved in 1848.

Our political currents and parties were not sufficiently clarified. There was no question of mutual sharing of political aims or a division of programs. None of the parties was organized on a sufficiently firm basis to pursue a definite goal or to exert firm pressure on Vienna. It was therefore no wonder that in the face of the radical sentiment of the people, the real leadership of the nation fell into the hands of the conservative or reactionary nobility. Our political program thus never progressed beyond passive opposition, which only masked the makeshift nature and immaturity of the underlying political reality.

Theoreticians of political science have differing opinions regarding the value of passive opposition. There are not too many concrete examples of the actual use of this tactic, and the specific situation in which we found ourselves was virtually unique. If I may express my own opinion, I believe passive opposition to be a political means that has no justification whatever. A consistent campaign of passive opposition is generally only the first step toward violent opposition; and it is my deepest conviction that political violence marks the beginning of the end. In reality, our refusal to participate in the government process was inconsistent and halfhearted, and in the end we gave it up altogether. Despite lengthy negotiations that we conducted with government representatives, we achieved no worthwhile political results through passive opposition. The abortive attempts to reach accommodation only emphasize the ineffectuality of our approach.

Whatever results we did achieve could have been secured without passive opposition, merely by the actual weight and influence that we had in the Austrian Empire. Not only did passive opposition fail to produce significant benefits, it did us actual harm. It deprived us of the opportunity for perfecting ourselves in parliamentary maneuvering, it encouraged political and intellectual indolence, it nourished authoritarianism.

I do not maintain that during the period of nonparticipation in government all of our thinking came to a halt, but obviously our intellectual and political life was drastically curtailed. Our political strategy during our revival was consistent with historically determined debility and exhaustion. The instability, indefiniteness, and disorganization of our literary renascence was paralleled by similar failings in our political practice. The policy of passive opposition was but a cloak designed to hide our shortcomings from ourselves and from the rest of the world. It was not until we launched our own active, virile political program that this threadbare cloak was discarded.

Because of our lack of readiness and the shortage of people qualified to play an active role in political life, large segments of the population came to look upon politics as our salvation and as a magic means of securing our rebirth. Many people were intrigued by the novelty of constitutional life, and political activity appeared as the ultimate pinnacle of national achievement. There could not have been a more grievous error. Just as in the time of Kollár we tended to undervalue the importance of political endeavor, so now we veered to the opposite extreme.

Political life does not have nearly the importance for a nation that is frequently ascribed to it. To put it more concretely: political independence will not save us. We were once independent and we lost our freedom, and there are independent nations in the world which nevertheless cannot call their soul their own. Palacký recognized that the political fate of our nation was dependent on what he called "the centralization of the entire globe." He continually pointed out that this trend toward world centralization leads to an ever greater need for cooperation with other nations and that under these conditions we will be able to maintain our identity only through unremitting work of enlightenment and cultural excellence. Our politicians as well as the rest of us have acted as if this voice were falling on deaf ears. We shall discuss the problem of small nations later; here we only wish to note its significance for contemporary political life.

Our renascence will be completed only after we have achieved a certain degree of political independence, for we will not be entirely alive until we are the masters of our own destiny. However, the achievement of this aim is becoming ever more difficult. Furthermore, political independence is not identical with spiritual and moral independence. Political life is only a modest part of the intellectual life of man and nation.

The Slavic Congress in Prague, 1848 / Austro-Slavism and its servile functions / Austro-Slavism pits Havlíček and Palacký against Russia in the name of free thought / The Polish uprising of 1863 / Pilgrimage to Moscow, 1867

In order to round out our political profile, we must also sketch the progress of the Slavic idea.

In the year 1848, the Slavic idea was to have proven itself from a practical viewpoint, and to some extent this expectation turned out to have been justified; the enthusiasm of our awakeners was not entirely wasted. The philologist and the military strategist—Šafařík and Jelačić—joined hands, and the first Slavic Congress was officially opened in Prague. The agenda of the Congress and its public statements seemed to contain the gist of Kollár's Slavic philosophy.

In a proclamation directed to the non-Slavic peoples of the Austrian Empire, it was "openly and solemnly" declared that the Slavs pledge loyal service to the ruling house and to the Austrian empire. In a manifesto to the nations of Europe, the Congress expressed its opposition to political Pan-Slavism and proclaimed allegiance to the principles of equality of all nations. In the name of liberty, equality, and fraternity, a friendly hand was extended to all neighbors. As they did a thousand years ago, the Slavs once again strove to ensure their own liberty and the liberty of other nations. The Slavs rejected the rule of pure force, noting that only Germans and Latin peoples relied upon the sword to achieve hegemony. The Slavic Congress demanded equal rights for all in the name of a noble humanism. The realm of the Austrian emperor was to be converted into a union of equal states. This is how Palacký formulated Kollár's ideas in his initial conception of the Austrian national federation.

At the conclusion of the first ceremonial session, Šafařík declared: "Either let us purify ourselves in action and prove that we are worthy of freedom, or let us convert ourselves at once into Germans, Hungarians, or Italians, so that we would no longer act as a burden to other nations and as a source of shame to our sons. Either let us achieve such a level of excellence that we can proudly say 'we are Slavs,' or let us cease to be Slavs altogether. A moral death is the worst kind of death. Freedom cannot be won without struggle. Either victory and a free nationhood, or honorable death."

The Congress broke up prematurely. In the subsequent storms Austro-Slavism speeded the demise of Slavic hopes. It had served its purpose.

After the Bach reaction and the installation of a constitutional system, the Austro-Slavism of the Slavic Congress was given an opportunity to establish itself firmly in the new parliament. But nothing happened.

Palacký's political program had its roots in these early constitutional beginnings. Palacký's *Idea of the Austrian State* corresponds to constitutional Austro-Slavism. From the year 1848, marking his first major public pronouncement in the letter to Frankfurt, Palacký propounded his idea in deliberate opposition to the universal hegemony of Russia. The strong intervention by Russia to suppress the Hungarian revolution shocked many hitherto Russophile Slavs.

The libertarian ideals of Havlíček and Palacký showed the Russian state and the Russian church in an unfavorable light. However, the reactionary reign of Bach and the unjust behavior of Vienna toward our people during the early days of constitutional reform changed the orientation of some of our leaders toward a more pro-Russian position. Havlíček declared that if he had no other choice but absolutism he would prefer the Russian type to the Austrian, and he tried to enlist Pan-Russianism on behalf of the Czech cause. He warned: "People who are concerned about a little bit of Pan-Slavism had better make sure that a much bigger threat is not on its way. Who can look into the future? The might of Slavdom is not harmful but beneficial to Austria, the Slavs give hope for continued support to the Austrian state."

The Polish uprising of 1863 somewhat weakened our sympathies toward Russia, and a distinction was made between the Russian state and the Russian people. The younger generation enthusiastically supported the Poles—the uprising symbolized the battle for our own freedom—while their elders defended legalism and rightly condemned the irresponsibility of the revolutionary aristocratic adventurers.

At this time, the Slavic festivities in Velehrad revived the Slavic idea in the Kollár's sense. The Cyril-Methodius concept of Slavism served the interests of Rome, and the Vatican was quite skillful in employing the Slavic idea for its own political advantage. However, even patriotic liberals attempted to exploit religious feelings in a nationalistic, Slavic sense. In fact, worshippers of verbal idols claimed to have found in the Cyril-Methodius idea the main meaning of our national development.

Then came the year 1867 and the pilgrimage to Moscow.

Much has already been written about this episode, and the affair no longer has contemporary relevance, so we need not analyze the polemics connected with it. Even Palacký admitted that the trip to Russia was most instructive. There is no doubt that much had been learned, but this only proves how little we have known about Russia, in spite of all our Russophilism. We still have very little information about Russia which is more accurate or extensive than that of Havlíček. The Congress ended in dissolution. Its most notable achievement was the emigration of a number of Czech peasant families to the Ukraine. No significant scholarly or literary connections were established as a result of the Congress.

Palacký's Idea of the Austrian State *after his trip to Russia / His Epilogue from the year 1872 / Palacký advocates Pan-Slavism and Russo-Czech alliance as shield against German and Hungarian domination / Politics of revival end on Russophile note*

At the time Palacký undertook his voyage to Russia he was recognized as the sole true leader of the nation. It is therefore highly significant that the Russian experience caused Palacký to alter the political program that he had conceived in 1848 and formulated in 1865 in his *Idea of the Austrian State.*

Whereas the Austro-Slavic formula initially meant "Austria against Russia," after Palacký's Moscow trip it became "Austria beside Russia."

Of course, the Russian pilgrimage was not the only reason for Palacký's shift of viewpoint. He had already softened his attitude toward Russia earlier, as was evident from his reaction to the Polish revolution. Furthermore, in his *Idea of the Austrian State*—in other words, as early as 1865—Palacký was impressed by the liberation of the Russian serfs. He wrote that "in the course of a single generation, the Russian people, hitherto virtually completely passive, will enter the world stage as an active power, in the tradition of ancient Slavic democracy."

Close acquaintance with the Russian scene had strengthened this opinion. In his Epilogue to *Radhošt* (1873), he discussed the matter in considerable detail. He declared that he still clung to his political program, namely, the idea of a federalized Austria. As he did in 1848, he still feared a universal Russian monarchy as "unspeakable evil" and a disaster "without measure or end." However, the focus of his attention had now shifted elsewhere. The events of 1866, marked by unjust and domineering German behavior, forced Palacký to make the following admission: "Unfortunately, even I am finally forced to abandon my belief in the permanence of the Austrian state. Not because such a continuation is impossible or undesirable, but because the Germans and Hungarians are destined to seize power and established a one-sided ethnic despotism. . . ."

Recalling his Russian experience, he continued:

I have already stated that I have little faith in the future of Austria, particularly in view of German and Hungarian despotism. We thus face the important question: what will become of the Slavs within the Austrian state, especially the Czechs? We cannot examine all the possibilities, and no mortal can predict the future. However, I say with full conviction that if the Czechs were ever to be forcibly incorporated into a Russian or Prussian empire, they would never accept such a fate. They would never forget that they have an ancient right to be governed only by a ruler chosen by themselves. They could not help but regard the Prussians—with their Germanizing fury—as implacable foes and murderers of their nation. With respect to the Russians, however, the situation would be quite different. Although the Czechs would refuse to become Russian subjects, they would regard the Russians as natural blood-relations, friends, and allies. They would be willing to serve as loyal partners, and—if need be—perhaps even act as the Russian vanguard in Europe.

In his dejection Palacký wished above all for European peace. He was convinced that "the idea of a federated Austria presupposed friendly relations with Russia as well as with other powers."

After the war of 1870 Palacký's fears of German aggressiveness mounted, and he looked to Russia for protection. German lust for power "cannot help but continually arouse and fortify Pan-Slavic sentiments, and enhance the mutual affection between Russians and Czechs."

In Palacký's mind Kollár's idea of Slavic reciprocity evolved into the more definitive and specific concept of a Russo-Czech alliance. The philosophy of revival thus completed the circle; it ended with the same Slavic idea with which it began, namely, pronounced Russophilism.

The Slavic idea in art and literature / The meaning of Havlíček's slogan: "Czech, not Slav" / Lack of true Slavic reciprocity / Erroneous theory of our role as East-West mediator

We have explored the political side of the post-Kollár period and showed its relationship to the ideas prevalent in Kollár's own time. Now, we will examine the relationship between the political evolution of the Slavic idea and the corresponding developments in literature, art, and general cultural life.

Here we naturally focus on Havlíček's credo: "Czech, not Slav." The impact of this slogan was not inconsiderable. After all, Havlíček was the first prominent Czech to have personal knowledge of Russia and Poland; he had lived in Moscow in Slavophile circles —how could his attitude fail to terrify our staunch patriots? Did it not smack of outright treason to the Slavic cause? Havlíček was not afraid to attack Tyl; he even dared to challenge Kollár.

When the dispute with Kollár broke out, a Slovak reader of *Slovan* published a polemic against Kollár, in which he unwittingly distorted Havlíček's position. Apparently, this reader was under the impression that Havlíček's "Czech, not Slav" slogan implied a denial of the existence of a common Slavic cultural heritage. In his reply, Havlíček clarified his position on this matter. He pointed out that "in order for us to become good Slavs, we must first cultivate the development of our own nation. The Slavic family will prosper only if its individual members—Czechs, Slovaks, southern Slavs, Poles, Russians—will brace themselves and engage in friendly competition."

Havlíček's article was directed against "an unfortunate practice common in Bohemia and Slovakia, whereby young men devoted themselves to the study of various Slavic languages without knowing the basic spelling rules of their own. Fantastic plans for a common language were enthusiastically discussed while fundamental education in our own language and culture was neglected." Havlíček did not deny the reality of Slavdom but tried to demonstrate that it was dependent upon the reality of its individual members.

When I proudly declare myself to be a Czech rather than a Slav, this cannot be interpreted to mean that I am ashamed of my Slavic heritage, but rather that I consider Slavism an ideal toward which we are progressing. In *practical* life it is impossible to make use of such an ideal, just as a hard-working person who expects ultimately to accumulate a sum of money cannot live on his *future* wealth. The awareness of a common origin and the need for fraternal ties is certainly not yet common among Slavic peoples. It is therefore obvious that it is one thing to strive for greater Slavic awareness by means of every-day, practical activity—and quite another thing to build a glorious Slavic edifice out of insubstantial dreams and visions, an edifice built on imaginary foundations. In brief, I have never done much talking about Slavism, but I have tried to behave like a Slav and *sit venia verbo*—like a Pan-Slav.

These words were not only valid for the time of Havlíček, they are true to this day. To the extent that Slavic reciprocity demands a knowledge of the Slavic world and a spiritual coexistence, our Slavism is still a wish rather than a reality. According to Kollár, Slavic reciprocity meant communion, interchange, and cultural integration. There was very little reciprocity in the past, and there is very little now; in fact, it is becoming rarer and rarer. Educated citizens of Prague or Petersburg are familiar with the latest novels of Parisian decadence, but they know nothing of real life in Russia nor in Bohemia. Even experts are grossly deficient in their Slavic background; so-called Slavicists abound who are totally ignorant of any language or literature but their own.

Acquaintance with Russian literature is far more widespread and thorough in Germany than in our own country. Germans, Frenchmen, and Englishmen are studying Russia and the rest of the Slavic world much more consistently and intensively than we do. That is the sad reality.

In this connection, I should remark about a theory that is being promulgated in our land as if it were the infallible truth—namely, that we Czechs are destined to mediate between the East and the West.

Actually, this theory has no substance. In the first place, we

Czechs do not directly border on the East (although the Slovaks do); our direct neighbors are the Germans and Poles, who also belong among Western peoples. More importantly, there is no task of cultural mediation that has been assigned to us. For example, the Russians always had much more direct ties with the Germans and the French than with us. Similarly, whatever literary or other influences the nations of Western Europe received from Russia they obtained directly, without any mediation. As mentioned previously, the Germans played a much more important role in this regard than we. To this day there is little more about Russia in our literature than what was written by Havlíček. We have no real history of Russia, for example, except for a small fragment that has recently been published. Similarly, the first history of Russian literature written by a Czech is just now being distributed. What, then, are we mediating—and to whom?

This situation is reflected not only in scholarly work but in literature, poetry, and art in general. Havlíček is our leading Slavic writer, Slavic not merely because he was a Czech but because he knew the Slavic world and felt it deeply. He was a genuine person, the kind of person who requires intimate knowledge of whatever he loves.

Our literature has not managed to elevate the Slavic idea beyond the abstract ideals of Kollár. To this day, the Slavic muse has not inspired our poets and writers to transcend the stage reached by Kollár.

New poetic and literary currents initiated by Byronism / The significance of Mácha / Hálek's continuation on path set by Mácha / The social involvement of our literature / Cosmopolitan tendencies / Popular realism

The influence of Byronism created new poetic and literary currents in our country. Mácha began the Byronic analysis of inner states and the portrayal of unusual, great men. His influence was felt as early as 1836, and he thus prepared the ground for the literary revolution of Havlíček.

Marjan Zdziechowski believed that Mácha represented a reaction against Kollár's Pan-Slavism. This view does not seem justified. Actually, in a sense Mácha continued along the path of Kollár, to the extent that both were dedicated to a humanist concept of man. Mácha's protest was directed against the distortion and degradation of man, a protest that became generalized through the political events of 1848. Kollár's rejection of Byronism, however, marked a significant difference from the attitude of Mácha.

Mácha's voice did not immediately silence the older patriotic trends. Mácha was alone, isolated, and ahead of his time. The political storms of 1848 and the subsequent period of reaction focused attention on more pressing problems, and it was only with the onset of constitutionalism and relative tranquility that the battle of Byronism against obsolete "patriotism" took up where Mácha had left it twenty years earlier.

This was not the first instance of delayed intellectual evolution in our lands, nor was it the last. Kollár extended the philosophy of Herder; Jungmann learned from Voltaire and even from Wieland. Similarly, toward the end of the 1850s Hálek resumed the work begun by Mácha.

We have never yet possessed a literature in the full sense of the term; that is to say, we have no firm and continuous literary tradition and consequently no literature that could evolve independently through its own resources. Our writers and intelligent readers are thoroughly at home in the German language and culture. They are in close intellectual contact with the literature of Germany and other European nations. There is a lag in our own literature, a delay before foreign models are assimilated and transformed. Our authors serve a mass readership but have very little influence on each other and on the world literary scene. For the same reasons, translations of foreign works generally have a greater influence than the original works of our own poets and writers. Jungmann's *Paradise Lost* is but one example of the translation activity of our most outstanding creative figures.

Hálek's Byronism had to wage a critical and polemical battle against obsolete patriotic tendencies, represented by such men as Malý—the same Malý who in his youth waxed enthusiastic over Kollár's *Slávy dcera*. A number of years earlier, Havlíček had to defend himself against the sarcasm of Malý; now, it was the turn of the young Byronists.

In order to understand the various concepts and controversies of the time, some explanation is in order. For this reason, I will summarize Hálek's essay from the year 1859, "On the Relationship between Czech Poetry and Poetry in General."

In essence, these are Hálek's ideas:

The subject of all poetry is *man*, man's life with all its varied circumstances. Those aspects of a poem which are exclusively Greek are understood by a Greek but not by man as man. Such poetry can educate Greeks but it can never educate men. It can inflame the passions of one nation or another and can increase the indolence of one nation or another, but it cannot enlighten mankind. A poet who is no more than a national poet is necessarily a mediocre one. Poetry is not limited by space or time, it knows no distinctions between peoples and lands.

It seeks men, and cares not where it finds them. . . . If a poet cannot abide the truth, it is not the fault of truth. And if any poet were to take it as his task to analyze the peculiarities of his own people, his task would soon be finished and he could accept the mantle of consummate national poet. But to analyze man—that is the work of eternity; it will be completed only when the pilgrimage of mankind through eternity has been completed. That is why being a poet for all men is so much more difficult than being a national poet. . . . The first task of poetry is to address man as man. . . . *Czech* poetry must never become the sole aim of our endeavor. Czech poetry has given excellent models for songs, for ballads, for minor narrative works; we have a right to be proud of these paradigms. But what then? Is this to be the total realm of our literary creation? What of drama? What of the novel? What of the epic? Has Czech literature created models for these forms as well? No. . . . The poet merely has to follow real life wherever it may lead him, and he can be sure he will not go astray. . . . Our credo can be stated thus: only poetic gifts, not nationalistic sentiments, can make a true poet. . . . In a few years, we shall clearly distinguish the true poet from the nationalistic versifier.

In the course of the bitter patriotic polemics customary in such matters, Neruda came to Hálek's aid with pithy vigor. In an afterword to Hálek's essay, Neruda wrote: "Yes—for us, the incessant jabbering about nation and fatherland is no longer of any interest whatever. From the bottom of my heart I detest anyone who believes that making patriotic pronouncements is a noble activity, and that such declarations absolve a man from the duty of actually *doing* anything for the nation. We have already reached such a level of education that there is no longer the slightest merit attached to merely being a patriot. It is certainly the first duty of every educated person to recognize his national allegiance, but that duty is an easy one. Now we must face the much more difficult task of elevating our nation to the level of world culture, to win universal recognition, and to ensure our continued national existence. This is what *cosmopolitanism* means. . . ."

Neruda's defense against the accusation of non-Slavism was equally terse and pointed: "Let us learn from other nations, let us recognize the level of their development, absorb their intellectual world. Then let us integrate all of this with the understanding we have imbibed with our mothers' milk and gathered from our native soil. We shall then create a new whole that will certainly be Slavic—for everything we do will necessarily have a Slavic stamp."

The essence of Hálek's and Neruda's position was realism. The two poets called for emphasis on the Czech man—and thereby Slavic man—but Czech man as he lived and breathed, rather than as archeology or abstract political theory would have him.

Hálek and Neruda therefore followed the populist direction of Havlíček. Hálek—the lesser poet of the two—as well as Neruda, achieved their greatest artistic moments when depicting Czech man: the man of the city, the worker, the farmer. Somewhat earlier, Božena Němcová had already discovered the Czech country folk in *Babička* (*Grandmother*), which was begun in the early fifties and published in 1855. In another work, *Báruška*, Němcová dealt with the question of the social role of women, servitude, and prostitution. A short time later, Světlá explored the woman's question in a broader context.

The first major novel of proletarian life also dates from this period: Pfleger-Moravský's *Z malého světa* (*From the Small World*), first published in 1863. Rudolf Mayer (1837–65) devoted his collection of poems *V poledne* (*At Noon*) to the working people. Most of these works were marred by an excess of abstract romanticism. Observation was too often replaced by fantasy and much that was false and distorted crept in. The writers of the time have not succeeded in ridding themselves of a certain cloying, old-fashioned patriotism, which makes a painful impression on the contemporary reader. This is especially true of Pfleger's novel.

Yet in spite of all these shortcomings, the "social" literature of the time represented a new force that complemented Havlíček's demand for universal suffrage. Neruda in particular portrayed certain Czech types with consummate mastery. He remains unsurpassed to this day as a Czech and Slavic poet; Slavic because Czech, and Czech because dedicated to our people and to their social concerns.

The majority of contemporary writers combined emphasis on social questions with a cosmopolitan eclecticism—a movement that proved irresistible to the younger generation. This is evident in Hálek, and to some extent even in Neruda. Foreign models alien to our life and needs were flooding our literature. As a result of these transplanted growths, mainly German and French, our Parnassus soon resembled a botanical garden rather than ground hallowed by the struggles of the Czech soul.

In the midst of this confused tangle of literature and life, the young generation launched its accusing *confiteor*—but this concerns the later stage of our development which we will discuss shortly.

In general, we have thus seen that the idea of nationality followed the same evolution in literature as it did in political and social life. The emphasis on patriotism and Slavism, based on abstract humanism and characteristic of the pre-Kollár and Kollár eras, receded. Instead, the younger writers, largely under the influence of Byronism, searched for the concrete Czech man. Naturally, they found him in purest form in the country and in those segments of the population least affected by the impact of culture. It was a healthy development, a movement directed toward the people, and nationality was conceived in populist terms. The definite, concrete, living essence of the Czech and Slavic was found in the people.

The Slavic idea in the graphic arts /Czech art dependent on foreign education and support / Patriotic painting not necessarily truly national / Czech and Slavic music

Developments in the graphic arts paralleled the general cultural trends, although the pattern was less clearly visible. The poor social status of artists, their dependence on foreign schools and foreign Maecenases made the paucity of our achievement in such areas as painting readily understandable. It is difficult to determine the truly Czech stylistic or conceptual elements in a work of a Čermák or even Mánes. A historical subject, even a patriotic subject, does not ipso facto ensure a work's genuinely national character.

Painters and other graphic artists were generally educated abroad and to a large extent lived abroad. The situation was different in music. We soon had a music that was truly Czech and, consequently, Slavic as well. This music was in itself a striking proof that we have real identity and that it was only a question of finding ourselves, as musicians such as Smetana had succeeded in doing.

The history of the Umělecká Beseda (Artistic Society), founded in 1863, is interesting and instructive. The fate of Smetana provides a telling example of the confusion of contemporary demands and lack of clarity regarding the essence of national art. We had a Czech music, we had a Slavic music, but we longed for something super-Slavic, Pan-Slavic. Only a few years ago, the air was still thick with pretentious speculations about Pan-Slavic music, as well as prescriptions for the composition of Pan-Slavic melodies. But no useful purpose is served in recalling these absurd chauvinistic excesses. Our gifted musicians found adequate guides in Czech folk songs to the national musical sensibility and had no need for grandiose supernational theories.

The Slavic idea in philosophy and science / *Philosophical trends of the time, under influence of German philosophy* / *The problems of Czech and Slavic philosophy; Augustin Smetana* / *Czech philosophy, too, oriented toward humanism and nationalism*

Philosophy and science may also be considered from a "national" viewpoint; even in precise scientific thought, national characteristics emerge not only in terms of subject but in terms of intellectual approach. English philosophy has a character totally different from its German counterpart. Even mathematics manifests itself differently in Russia, let us say, than in Germany. Russian authors have amply dealt with these matters, but in our country such questions have not even been formulated as yet.

From the very beginning of our revival, our leading thinkers drew heavily on German philosophy. Kollár's case is especially relevant, and others followed Kollár's example of utilizing German philosophy as a basic ideological foundation. Palacký, for example, was greatly indebted to Kant. Kantian philosophy is implicit in Palacký's historical work, in his ethical opinions (categorical imperative), in his religious outlook (antirationalism), and his political credo (eternal peace, nonviolence). As a Kantian, Palacký was not only more profound than Kollár but more progressive as well. Havlíček's philosophy was concerned through all his life with theological problems; it was expressed in *Epištoly Kutnohorské* (*Epistles from Kutná Hora*). Havlíček's views of state and society were influenced by the freethinking philosophers of the revolutionary era, such as Voltaire and Rousseau, as well as Bolzano and the Russian thinkers. In general, however, Havlíček was a typical representative of the philosophy of healthy common sense; here, too, Havlíček consistently showed his close tie to the people.

In common with Havlíček, the majority of our philosophers conceived of their discipline in opposition to religion and church, in the tradition of the historical development of the Czech reformation. As mentioned earlier, in Palacký's time systematic, formal philosophy was primarily German. In addition to Kant, Hegel and Herbart exerted great influence. During the period of reaction Herbart virtually became the official philosopher of the Austrian Empire. Needless to say, the professors of Prague University also had significant impact, especially Leonhardi and his successors.

As early as 1848, the principal problems of Czech philosophy were annunciated by Augustin Smetana. The name Smetana, at last, had a good ring in Bohemia—but Augustin Smetana had richly deserved recognition a long time previously.

Like Kollár, Smetana believed that the cultural leadership of mankind was shortly to be bestowed upon the Slavs. We Czechs were destined to take the first step by mediating between East and West. Smetana's concept of the East included not only Russia but also Asia.

According to Smetana, just as classical culture ended with the decadence of the Greeks and Romans, so the Germano-Latin hegemony was coming to an end and a Slavic era was dawning. It was the task of the Slavs to preserve the intellectual achievements elaborated by the West. Specifically, we Czechs were given the duty of safeguarding German culture, of ordering and disseminating the treasures of German civilization. In Smetana's view, we were destined to transmit the products of German genius to future generations of thinkers and creators. Smetana considered his own work to mark the end of German cultural superiority and the initiation of the Slavic cultural era.

Like many other Czechs, Smetana was totally immersed in German philosophy, especially that of Hegel. He recognized, however, that it was desirable for our thought to take a different direction. Smetana believed that the nineteenth century was the period of humanism par excellence. Under our leadership, rationalistic indifference to spiritual life would be overcome through art, and an unjust social order would be conquered through humanism and love. Smetana realized that the social question was urgent—it was at the very core of our cultural existence. Philosophy as taught by the Germans would disintegrate, its parts would be absorbed into other disciplines. The cultural transition that we Czechs were to initiate and lead could only be accomplished by means of peaceful cooperation with Germans. In the interests of this task and in response to the demands of humanism, he called for fraternal relations between the two nations living in our lands.

Smetana quite aptly defined the problem of Czech philosophy and the Czech spirit. His vision of the humanist aim of philosophical renascence was a noble one. He perceived that an organic bond with the past must necessarily include a solution of the social question. He thus completed the humanist theory of Kollár and provided a philosophic framework for the social and popular aspirations of our intellectual leaders. His remarks about the Slavic aspects of our philosophy are also noteworthy. It is worth pondering how this good Czech wished to end German cultural dominance: through self-sacrifice on our part. This was to be the last in a series of sacrifices the Czech people have made for the sake of German culture over the centuries—and it was to be a conscious, deliberate, free act on our part.

Czech scholarship and education / The establishment of Czech secondary and technical schools / Cultivation of science along practical lines / A school system befiting the nation of Komenský

During the period under consideration, our progress in the various disciplines derived mainly from the establishment of a Czech secondary school system, followed somewhat later by technical schools.

This development is an important one for the understanding of the role of science in our national life.

Secondary schools, especially after the reforms of 1848, offered not only general education in the humanities but also instruction of a vocational and practical nature. Secondary schooling was at the heart of our educational program, and received most of our pedagogical attention. As a result, the character of our scholarly literature was popular rather than strictly scientific. This was in organic harmony with the popular tendencies of the period.

The practical and consistent nature of these developments was also evident from the fact that the establishment of technical schools received top priority in the development of the educational system. In the Middle Ages, the University of Prague was the first one in Eastern Europe. Our first technical school was founded in Prague, and our higher education took a practical rather than a theoretical form. At the German university, the first chairs in which Czech was the language of instruction also had practical characters; the faculties of medicine, law, even philology, and history primarily served the needs of secondary education.

Since we did not have a complete university, in terms of basic philosophical and scientific foundations, we were still dependent on German scholarship. This dependence was aggravated by a lack of scholarly books, especially textbooks. We failed to undertake an organized, systematic program of translation, demonstrating that the orientation of our scholarly endeavor toward popular needs had its negative aspect: namely, the significance of the exact sciences and of philosophy was not sufficiently appreciated. We are the nation of Komenský. We took our educational system seriously, but no more so than other nations who never had a Komenský. In view of our heritage it behooves us to surpass other nations in the quality of our educational system, in the excellence of our philosophy, arts, and sciences. Education must be our foremost national and political concern—this is the legacy of Komenský and of the Bohemian Brethren; this is the aim of our humanist enlightenment. Above all, what matters is not the number of schools but their quality. The educational policy of the nation of Komenský must set an example to the world. If education is what makes a man human, reform of education must be the concrete goal of our humanistic striving.

Humanism as a goal requires humanistic means / The question of national tactics: not violence, but enlightenment, education, knowledge / Palacký's formulation

And now let us face the heart of the matter.

All the significance of our history is encompassed in this imperative: let us fulfill our humanist goals through moral and intellectual excellence. We must understand with our minds and hearts that pure humanism must not be merely a slogan of national revival but that the striving of Dobrovský, Kollár, and Havlíček must become the striving of one and all, that humanism as a goal and national program must consistently determine our national tactics.

How are we going to survive as an independent nation? Our history as well as current developments are forcing us to come to a clear understanding of this question: how can a small nation survive and remain independent?

This question tormented our awakeners. It disturbed Dobrovský. All of Kollár's labor was directed toward finding the means of overcoming our inherent smallness. Palacký transposed Kollár's solutions from the realm of culture to that of politics. And of course Palacký could answer the question of how a small nation can survive no more satisfactorily than Kollár; after all, politics, like all practical sciences, depends upon theoretical principles. But if humanism is the ultimate aim of all our thought, it must also be the ultimate goal of our political activity. We will achieve humanism only through humanistic means—enlightened heads and warm hearts.

Reminders of our numerous historical battles for existence—the uprising ending with the defeat on the White Mountain, our decline, our revival during the French Revolution and eighteenth-century enlightenment, the revolution of 1848, the Polish uprising—all this impels the thoughtful Czech to ponder: violence or nonviolence, the sword or the plow, blood or sweat, death or life?

Not with violence but with love, not with the sword but with the plow, not with blood but with work, not with death but with life—that is the answer of our Czech genius, the meaning of our history and the heritage of our great ancestors.

I have already remarked on Palacký's testament, in which he opposed violence and recommended peaceful tactics. Havlíček held the same opinion, and so did Kollár. It could not have been otherwise. This question of national tactics is not only enormously important but also enormously complicated, full of enigmas and problems. We shall try to address ourselves to some of these questions somewhat later. Now, I shall merely quote the words of Palacký which he uttered as director of the society Svatobor in 1864, at the time he was about to formulate his overall political program. The speech was published in the annual report of Svatobor for 1864–65. The essential point, presented below, is as relevant to our present discussion as though it had been especially written for that purpose:

It is generally agreed that it was the Czech writers who kept this nation from dying, who nourished it and formulated noble goals for its inspiration. It is recognized that literature became the real fountain-head of national life.

Therefore, our writers became the awakeners, teachers, and leaders on the nation's spiritual journey. . . .

Our nation is small, both in numbers and in the size of its territory. For more than a thousand years it had to struggle for its existence against a mightier neighbor. I have explained elsewhere that our entire history is characterized by a continual struggle between Slav and German, Slavism and Germanism, in virtually all areas of human endeavor. I believe every child knows by now that in this fateful struggle we emerged not merely honorably but even gloriously, in spite of the inequality of numbers and material power.

But there is another aspect of our history which is still not generally appreciated and which requires emphasis: whenever we emerged victorious, it was primarily because of spiritual superiority rather than physical power, and whenever we were defeated the fault always lay in a lack of our spiritual strength, moral courage, and stamina.

It is woefully wrong to believe that the military miracles of our Hussite ancestors were accomplished by brawling, tattered savages—as our ancestors are too often portrayed. Rather, these victories resulted from spiritual and moral superiority, from the high ideals and enlightenment of our people. On the other hand, when we succumbed two centuries later and virtually sank into our grave, we were punished for trying to compete with our neighbors not with spiritual might but with brute force. We matched our foes only in moral decay. During the past two hundred years we have existed only physically, our spirit had departed; and when it showed itself now and then, it manifested itself in a foreign garb. The world had thus forgotten us as if we no longer existed. And now, as we are coming back to life and beginning to claim our right to existence, many people are surprised; it seems to them as if we were doing something wrong and unseemly. To the extent that we can now claim our place in the family of nations with full justification and good conscience, we can do so, not on the grounds of our size and material resources, but as a consequence of the spiritual strength and moral courage of those who had preceded us in the struggle for national revival. From the very beginning, those pioneers fortified themselves with true enlightenment, true selflessness, and purity of character. Otherwise they would not have been able to withstand the many enormous difficulties in their path. Because of the moral and spiritual excellence of these men even our foes had to admit that our aims and deeds were honorable and not deserving of condemnation or violent resistance. Our national awakening was made possible only by such means. It is a well-known maxim that every movement can maintain itself in power only through those methods that gave it birth. For this reason, our writers and other spiritual awakeners and leaders have the duty to excel in their education, dedication, and character. In fact, the moral virtues, intelligence, and courage of our leaders must clearly surpass those of our enemies, who are trying to destroy our national existence. We will succeed in permanently securing our future only if the age-old struggle that God has assigned to us will be fought with weapons forged by the spirit.

I know very well what a great and difficult task this is. But I also know that it is not impossible of fulfillment. The good Lord has bestowed the elements of wonderful qualities on the Czech spirit. If our blood is less cool and settled than that of other peoples, our mind is correspondingly more alert, fresh, and fine. All we need is a steady and courageous will guided by reason. After all, we have already proved to the world once that we are capable of surpassing other nations in spiritual excellence, if we but devote all our will and endurance to the task. Of course, such an achievement requires freedom, too; this is why we failed so often in the past. But now we must recognize that our fetters have been removed or greatly loosened. Our humanist and nationalist endeavors, provided they eschew subversive tendencies, are no longer fraught with obstacles. Reactionary countermoves are of course always possible, but their duration and effect will be reduced by the fervor of our spiritual dedication. Galileos were always capable of rising to the required heights, even under conditions of greatest tyranny....

The only purpose and meaning of my speech is to remind our compatriots—particularly the younger generation that is about to join us in our battle—where our gaze should be directed, what our true aims and aspirations should be. It is not enough for us to produce books to keep our nation from dying of intellectual starvation. We have a more serious task: if we do not raise our own spirit and the spirit of our nation to a higher level than that of our neighbors, we will not only fail to secure an honorable place in the family of nations but we will finally lose the right to our national existence. That is why it is the duty of every Czech writer to make the fruits of his mind surpass in their inner worth the products of other languages and cultures. It is the special duty of the young to prepare as early and as intensively as possible to compete against the best of foreign rivals, in science as well as in the arts.

In certain respects I disagree with Palacký's view of our historic development. Nevertheless, I believe with all my heart that his words point out the most efficacious tactics for our nation to follow.

One-sidedness of the historicist approach to the national work of enlightenment / The present and the future—not the past—must be the subjects of our concern

We maintain that to be true to our heritage we must regard the work of education and enlightenment as our national way of life; we must seek our salvation in knowledge and in science. However, before we can embark on this enterprise we must identify and delimit the individual disciplines of our study, as well as the methods and directions of our intellectual pursuits. Elsewhere, I have submitted some of my thoughts in this regard, and with God's help I hope to carry these ideas further. Here we will explore one intellectual current that has characterized our national striving throughout the period of revival. I am referring to that peculiar historicism, that archeological method of perception that Havlíček combatted and of which he accused Kollár. This tendency toward historicism was also typical of Palacký.

History is a great teacher, and this is especially true in our case.

Certainly, we have learned much from history—but the supreme teacher is the present, actual life itself. And there is no point in denying that we are still drawn away from the present and toward the past more than we need and that this preoccupation poses a serious danger to our national cause. Šafařík and Kollár turned our attention one-sidedly toward the remote Slavic past. Palacký corrected this imbalance somewhat, by concentrating on our specific Czech history. But above all we need to grasp the present, and Palacký's influence is not altogether beneficial in this regard. Palacký's historicism has led many of our best people toward sterile conservatism.

To express the matter somewhat differently—our perspective is distorted to the extent that history and historical scholarship constitute the main force of our national consciousness. Up to a point this is of course a natural and understandable development. However, we must correct our overemphasis on history by a greater concentration on the disciplines that inform us about the world of the present and the future, in other words, the natural and social sciences. We have an aptitude for such studies, as evidenced by names such as Rokytanský, Škoda, Purkyně. But these men wrote in a foreign tongue, and it is our task to make their work truly our own, to incorporate it into our national awareness.

There is no question that our gaze is still directed backward. It is significant that to this date we still lack a history of the post-White Mountain period, of the more recent past; this is the extent to which we are fascinated by our past. Similarly, our art emphasizes figures derived from the dim past, as if only our ancient forefathers were worthy of fame. We are inclined to see only our great past.

As I said, this attitude is understandable and legitimate up to a certain point; but it is one-sided, incomplete. We must penetrate behind the mysterious veil of the present; we must come to understand current life and its conditions. Such an understanding, supplemented of course by a proper historical background, will give us the orientation and assurance to look boldly into the future.

That is our great task. We are on the right path. Palacký was still preoccupied by the past, and this gave his politics a conservative character. But Havlíček had already admonished us to turn to the living present and to derive our national strength from a firm grasp of reality. In theory, Palacký admitted as much, as we will shortly demonstrate, but Havlíček was more thorough and energetic in living up to this principle. His commitment to this principle became evident during his dispute with Kollár. One lively Slavic lad, said Havlíček, is worth more than all the old Slavic divinities who were or will be dug up, cast or will be cast. Havlíček expressed everything in these words; our own lives are more important for future generations, and far nearer, than the lives of our misty ancestors.

This attitude is relevant not only to politics but also to our entire individual and national existence. It is the philosophical basis of an outlook that may be called "realism." I tried to formulate it in an abstract and scholarly way in my *Konkrétní logika* (*Concrete Logic*). The central imperative of this philosophical approach may be put this way: always strive to understand everything in its concrete reality, by going to its core. The first intellectual requirement is to understand things as they are, rather than to analyze processes of change and development. Naturally, the quality of any phenomenon is affected by its evolution, but attention must not be focused exclusively on historical change per se. Historicism often has an unwholesome effect even on individual personal character. A person lost in the stream of continual change becomes vague and indecisive in responding to the needs of every-day life.

The past should be subordinated to the present, although the past of course illuminates the present. For example, through a careful study of Kollár we can see our entire past in a meaningful way— the perspective of the present makes the past significant. Ever since I have begun to think about the Czech question, I have tried to focus on our actual life and our actual circumstances. Our history and ancient monuments were only significant to me as corroboration of current sociological observations. I have tried to follow my own path in these studies; I turned to others, mainly Havlíček and Palacký, only when I needed confirmation of my own findings. In contrast, historical empiricism has no such anchor in present reality; at best, it seeks to derive its convictions from the past and portrays reality as a mosaic of quotations from authorities of the past.

The two approaches just discussed apply to all intellectual work. The so-called historical influence may be nothing more than a mechanical acceptance of certain historical facts—or it may be a living force that flows organically from meticulous observation and analysis. Otherwise, history is not a teacher but merely a policeman.

The ideas of Purkyně, supplementing the historicism of Palacký /
The struggle for an encyclopedia / Palacký recognized the
importance of modern science for the national cause: his plans
for the popularization of science / Palacký and Havlíček
favored "realistic" education

The limitations of our secondary school system, particularly its overemphasis on classical education and on history, became increasingly evident. Purkyně was well aware of this problem, as is clear from his plans for a Czech Academy and for the popularization of science, especially natural science. These plans still have not been realized, even though they are feasible and address themselves to a pressing need.

But even Palacký, the main pillar of historicism, came to recognize its shortcomings. Palacký's admission in this regard is revealing.

The lack of a popular base in the scientific disciplines was evident to our thinkers for some time. Jungmann had been painfully aware of the paucity of scientific literature in the Czech language. He urged Marek to provide us with works on metaphysics and philosophy, and he contemplated the preparation of a popular encyclopedia of general knowledge. Jungmann was inspired by the French encyclopedists, including his mentor Voltaire. At the same time, this point of view reflected a real, specific national need. Actually, the most fitting model for Jungmann's plans was Komenský, with his pansophic method. Jungmann was not well acquainted with Komenský; the fact that he came to the same conclusion as his illustrious predecessor supports my contention that historical development is governed by the changing needs of reality—in this case, the need for comprehensive education.

Palacký, too, concerned himself with projects for an encyclopedia. His first proposal dates from the year 1829. Initially, Palacký thought more in terms of a conventional dictionary than an encyclopedic compendium of scientific knowledge. His ideas gradually matured and deepened; I believe that this was largely because of a growing appreciation of Komenský.

In 1850 Palacký once again took up the question of an encyclopedia and submitted his proposal to the Matice Česká (an organization supporting arts and sciences). Palacký's attitude toward history as compared to the natural sciences is of special interest. As far as exact science was concerned, Palacký was content to present only brief summaries. On the other hand, the disciplines that were historical and thus "moral in the broadest sense" were to be given much more extensive treatment. "Astronomy, mathematics, and physics would be presented far more concisely than history, literature, and the biography of great men. The political sciences would be given considerable scope, corresponding to the requirements of current life."

Within two years, however, Palacký changed somewhat in his approach to the content and orientation of the encyclopedia. One of its main functions had now become to acquaint the public with the results of modern science, particularly natural science:

If ever nations felt the need for education and enlightenment, now that the face of the world has assumed a new form through the invention of the steam engine and mechanical transportation, popular knowledge has become a vital necessity for our nation. In other words, the utilization of modern science has become of vital national importance.

Through the miraculous power of steam and electricity, the world situation has taken on new dimensions, old barriers between lands and nations are disappearing, all tribes and races of mankind have drawn closer together. Under such circumstances, the isolated individual is becoming relegated more and more to the realm of fairy tales. At the same time, competition among nations has been awakened to a degree heretofore unknown, and it is ever growing. A nation failing to compete successfully with its neighbors will surely perish. I therefore ask whether our own nation—endowed by God with magnificent gifts of the spirit—has the right to squander these gifts through apathy and indecision. Can we afford to withdraw from a contest when only full participation can assure us of a right to future existence?

But let us descend from the realm of abstractions and generalities to bare, concrete reality; this address will thereby gain in clarity. It is high time for our nation to awaken and to orient itself in the spirit of the modern world. It is time for our nation to lift its gaze beyond the narrow bounds of the fatherland and, without lessening our patriotic fervor, to become an attentive, conscientious citizen of the world. We, too, must take part in world commerce and share in the general progress. Without abandoning our ancient faith and honesty, we must give up our old, ingrained apathy, our age-old laxity and indolence, which are the reasons for our poverty and depression. We must embark upon a new path to invigorate our land through industrialization, benefiting not only manufacturers, traders, and artisans but also farmers, craftsmen, and clerical workers. The old inexpensive, comfortable life has departed for ever, but so has the crudity and the lack of the pleasant goods and customs of civilization. Naturally, public taxes will rise, regardless of the kind of government we may have. If we are not to become stunted and impoverished, we must triple our zeal and pull ourselves up to the level of other nations, which through their enterprise rule the vast reaches of the world.

Against the objection that these tasks of enlightenment should be performed by textbooks and that no encyclopedia could achieve miracles, Palacký pointed out that special circumstances call for special measures, among which he included the encyclopedia. "Our people may excel others in gentility, manners, love, and capacity for learning—but the fact remains that in terms of intellectual power and spiritual breadth we are still behind our neighbors. Our nation suffers, so to speak, from a lack of intellectual sustenance, a lack of material that could nourish, train, and improve the mind."

We thus see that the movement toward popularization was becoming dominant even in the area of science. Palacký correctly charted the means whereby we would gain a truly cosmopolitan, universal outlook and thereby offset our inherent smallness, of which Kollár and other awakeners were so painfully aware. And here Komenský gave us the best guide, by his prescription that even the most profound metaphysical knowledge should be formulated with such economy and clarity that eight-year-old children could understand it.

It is especially noteworthy that Palacký recognized the national significance of "realistic" (*reální*) education as against a humanist-historical one. He made some fascinating comments about this question in his Epilogue. He stated that one reason why he and his friends, in the time of Emperor Francis I, were stressing disciplines that were "concrete or realistic" was a purely political one; people dedicated to the political sciences might have been accused of subversive tendencies, whereas a study of natural science could have no conspiratorial or revolutionary implications. Thus, through its bureaucratic short-sightedness, which forbade the study of political science and fostered emphasis on "practical" disciplines, the old Austrian regime of Francis I actually helped bring about its own destruction. As has been repeatedly demonstrated, a significant democratic element is implicit in the natural sciences.

It is certainly true that political studies, carried out by means of obsolete scholastic methods, may have led to little more than grandiose dreaming and confused thought. Havlíček sensed this extremely well. Incensed by some of the more fantastic statements of radical compatriots, he delivered his well-known plea: away with all idealism—that is to say, fantasy—and hold fast to reality.

The realistic movement of our own days is closely connected with the realism of Havlíček and Palacký, although nowadays the emphasis upon natural science no longer plays such a dominant role.

Journalism as a literary instrument of revival / The powerful influence of Czech journalism on public opinion / Journalism as a natural organ of popular movements

In our survey of the intellectual climate during the era of Palacký, we cannot help but mention our journalism. To a considerable extent journalism represents the modern method of intellectual work. We think telegraphically and stenographically; we want our information to be brief, concise, and yet broad. We want to know everything: the small, the great, the important, the trivial. The journalist must therefore be laconic and assume a broad general education on the part of his readers. The journalist himself must of course have such an educational background himself to a remarkable degree—otherwise he is a mere "jour-naliste" in the true sense of the word, a day laborer; worse yet, without proper education he is an hour-laborer, a minute-laborer, an ephemera.

On the other hand, a cultivated newspaperman, one who matches the high educational level he expects of his reader, is a modern master of style and an intellectual virtuoso.

Journalism played an exceptionally important role in our lands from the very beginning, since we did not possess as rich a heritage of books and journals as other nations. And we have had some excellent journalists. In German, they presented our case to the world; in Czech, they served our own people. Palacký was a journalist. Havlíček was a journalist of such excellence that he could well be the envy of other nations. How we long for that time when Czech newspapermen will once again seek instruction and inspiration from Havlíček! Unfortunately, as soon as Havlíček stepped aside, the new parliamentary era and the hectic political life of Vienna induced our younger journalists to follow foreign models, particularly Viennese. As a result, the level of our journalism steadily declined, just as the quality of our literature has so often deteriorated as a result of a too unimaginative dependence upon foreign models.

Because of a scarcity of scholarly and scientific literature and the great need for popular education, our journalism gained great authority and respect among the people. This is one of the reasons why Havlíček had such fresh, direct impact, as compared to the influence of more learned, scholarly men such as Palacký.

Hálek, Neruda, and Sladkovský are among those who tried to follow in the footsteps of Havlíček, but they never reached his eminence. The free-thinking newspapers, especially *Národní listy*, dominated public opinion. Journalism had become the literary organ of the popular, democratic movement.

It is not coincidental that Barák is considered a friend of the workers and students. *Národní listy* had a great and deserved influence on the younger generation, particularly the students. This influence was all the more significant as the majority of students had to attend the German university. Czech journalism thus assumed the spiritual guidance of patriotically oriented youth.

Gradually, the quality of Old Czech journalism declined, followed by a similar decline in newspapers adhering to the Young Czech party, with a concomitant loss of influence. There was great hunger for newspapers and their number was constantly increasing, but at the expense of depth and cultural level. Literary and journalistic parvenus gradually entrenched themselves. It is the first task of our current crop of newspapermen to eliminate this clique and to restore our journalism to its former eminence.

CHAPTER 5

The Mind of
František Palacký

In the foreword to the last volume of his *Dějiny národa
českého* (*A History of the Czech Nation*), Palacký—reviewing this
major work of his life—concisely outlined the core of our historical
experience: alone and "perhaps prematurely," the Czechs—a small
nation—took upon themselves a great task, to wrest the human
spirit free of medieval authority. They were twice forced to wage
great battles for this cause. The first great war was the Hussite
struggle, by which Czechs won acceptance for their religious beliefs. The Czechs took up arms a second time during the Thirty-
Years War, but this time they were defeated and their reformation
was violently suppressed. "From this time on," wrote Palacký, "a
false idea has been gaining credence, namely, that Czech history of
the fifteenth and sixteenth centuries was largely an unfortunate
aberration worthy only of shame. All-embracing, merciless reaction snatched away all the spiritual monuments of that epoch. Writings from the period were labeled dangerous poison, searched out
and destroyed over the course of the entire subsequent century.
Whatever escaped by chance the onslaught of savage fanaticism ultimately succumbed to the indifference of later generations."

From Tomáš G. Masaryk, *Palackého idea národa českého* (Prague, 1926).
First published in *Naše Doba*, Vol. V (1898), pp. 769–95.

Under such sad circumstances, when the dominant idea was to drown our history in a sea of forgetfulness rather than disturb the peace and tranquility of a later time, Palacký undertook his life work: to write his nation's history and, in particular, to render an account of the Hussite period, for "it is extremely important to present this pinnacle of Czech history in a deeper, more intelligent way than was done heretofore."

Palacký hoped that a proper presentation of its history, notably the epoch of its greatest achievement, would help arouse the nation. After all, "even in the darkest period of its decline, the nation continued to yearn for its past glory, turning its gaze upon history as if it were a blessed anchor in the midst of a lethal storm." Of course, Palacký also hoped that his life's work, "ended but not completed," would be carried on by younger historians and extended into more recent times. "I pray from the bottom of my soul that this beloved nation of ours—sorely tried beyond all others—will soon be given a true mirror of its entire past, for its edification, awakening, and invigoration, so that it will always walk along the paths of truth and righteousness, without overweening pride in prosperity and without faint-heartedness in adversity."

We will not achieve such edification and invigoration through the knowledge of isolated historical facts and details but only through grasping their significance. The great historians of the world have not gained fame merely by unearthing documents and recounting events but by interpreting the meaning of such documents and events. Similarly, the greatness of Palacký derived from his ability to tell us the significance of our history for our nation and for the world. He was able to grasp its meaning, its "idea," to use Palacký's own expression.

Even if Palacký had not expressly pointed out the summit of our historical evolution, readers of Czech history—no matter how indolent—could not help but ponder the striking fact that our entire historical development from Charles IV to the end of the eighteenth century was dominated by a religious idea. In the reign of Charles IV the Reformation movement began; it culminated, as Palacký noted, in the Hussite period. The Thirty-Years War represented a decline from this pinnacle—but the content of this period of decline was still the same, it was still religious, and this religious concern was evident all the way to the end of the eighteenth century. The year 1775 was still marked by stormy religious upheavals that forced Maria Theresa to yield. Finally, Joseph II proclaimed religious freedom.

Thus, during four centuries of our history, the leading idea was a religious one. This idea constitutes the essence of our history; it exhausts the meaning of our past.

Of our past only? Is it possible that our nation has now embarked upon an entirely new course from that followed over the preceding four centuries? Is it possible that a nation could live with a double soul? No. Our so-called revival is a natural and logical extension of our early past; notably, it is a link with the ideas and ideals of our reformation. Of course, it is an incomplete link and we are not yet fully aware of its nature. Our rebirth has not yet been achieved; we are still far from properly utilizing our history for our enlightenment, awakening, and invigoration as Palacký had hoped. But to some extent we have already profited from our history; we have become aware of the significance of our struggle for the religious regeneration of mankind. Dobrovský, Kollár, Šafařík, Palacký, Havlíček, Augustin Smetana—these men have striven all their lives to clarify for us the tremendous and daring crusade that our ancestors launched when embarking upon the reformation. The leading idea of our revival is the idea of our reformation. The circumstances have changed, some of the details and outer forms are different, but the meaning and the goal have remained the same. To clarify and to present this goal was Palacký's life work. His program was to explain the significance of our national striving. Palacký's program did not consist in any particular constitutional proposal or in any particular new proposal in the language question. We have to find Palacký's program in his "work of a life-time," his interpretation of our history.

Philosophy of Czech history; the Bohemian Brethren

If the leading idea of our history was the religious question, this does not mean that the Czech question was entirely confined to theology. Palacký himself showed otherwise.

As Palacký was completing his history of the Hussite movement, Hoefler—an adherent of the clerical party—condemned that glorious epoch in the contemptuous manner typical of our ancient antagonists. Palacký subsequently wrote a pamphlet directed against Hoefler (*Die Geschichte des Hussitenthums und Prof. Höfler*, 1867), which became "an apologia for Hus and his followers." And in this apologia Palacký declared that as a historian he was not only concerned with the theological aspect of the movement but with its moral and national significance: "Did this movement really have a moral meaning and justification or not?"

In posing this question regarding the most crucial period of our history, Palacký naturally first had to clarify for himself the basic question of religion. He did this quite early, even before he undertook his work in history.

In the early articles on aesthetics (beginning in 1820), Palacký presented his main philosophic concepts. In particular, he explained his fundamental approach to religion, which can be summed up as follows.

The foundation and ultimate goal of human striving is "godliness." Godliness is regarded by Palacký as "a certain harmony with God and resemblance to divine attributes; in other words, participation in the nature of God, and the image of God in man." This is not only a symbolic, formal scheme but the real force and goal behind all spiritual life. . . .

This idea underlies Palacký's history of the Czech nation. He regards the spiritual maturing of mankind and of individual nations in terms of gradual realization of the religious ideal. Like other modern historians and philosophers of history, Palacký saw the history of each particular nation as the gradual unfolding of its own particular spiritual life. How our nation succeeded in this task is the core of Palacký's historical writing. In the pamphlet directed against Hoefler, Palacký briefly explained his philosophy of Czech history.

He pointed out that by nature, a human being needs faith and reason. As in all other fields, so in religion, too, decisions are made either by authority or by independent reason. All human thought and desire is determined by the conflict between authority and free thought. Authoritarian religion typically developed into Catholicism, whereas Protestantism represents the type of religion that emphasizes rationality. Protestantism was a natural outgrowth and antagonist of Catholicism. Palacký was convinced that pure Christian teaching was sufficient for men of all levels of education and for all time, and that this pure teaching was impaired by Catholicism. The breach took two forms. The church hierarchy, progressively seizing all ecclesiastic authority, placed undue emphasis upon dogma and neglected the moral conduct of life. In a manner similar to that of Tolstoy, Palacký showed that Christ's teaching was extremely simple, both from the speculative, theological side and from the practical, moral side. At the same time, this teaching was noble, popular, and, above all, seminal. It was not opposed to reason; on the contrary, it was the highest manifestation of reason. But since every doctrine needs special organs for its protection and propagation, a special class of religious teachers arose, namely, the priests. As could be expected the existence of a priesthood affected the subsequent development of doctrine in an anthropomorphic manner. And it was anthropomorphism that distorted Christ's message in the Middle Ages. At first, the ecclestiastical hierarchy in Rome emphasized its role as teacher of the faithful, but soon it perverted Christ's word in order to gain secular power reminiscent of ancient Rome. Christ's demand for the love of God and man continually receded before an ever more complicated dogma. Love became less important than the analysis of complex theological theories. Christ's longing for a heavenly kingdom was essentially the same phenomenon as the yearning for the infinite described by contemporary philosophy. It certainly involved no abstract or abstruse dogma. The Roman hierarchy ruled over the Christian world, and its popes were on the verge of becoming a species of Christian Dalai Lamas. Fortunately, Christianity contained within itself its own cure: free reason.

The second violation of pure Christianity perpetrated by Catholicism was neglect of morality, leading to moral decay.

Opposition within the church itself was not sufficient to correct this two-fold distortion of true Christianity. It was necessary for a segment of Christianity to take a stand outside of the ruling church; this was the providential mission of Protestantism, particularly our Czech Reformation. The Roman church was opposed by a new church that proclaimed the supremacy of free reason bound only by the authority of the Bible.

The Christian world was split in two. In this religious and ecclesiastical dualism (it is significant that in his most intimate moods Palacký did not consider the Orthodox church), Palacký saw a great, redeeming historical development. According to Palacký this development was in accord with the dualism of the human spirit. Some are endowed with an active temperament, others with a more passive one. Some are independent, others follow a leader; some resist authority, others require it. This natural law of polarization that brings about the male-female duality in all organic beings is reflected in matters of church and religion by Protestantism and Catholicism.

Though Palacký regarded sixteenth-century Protestantism as an essential step in the evolution beyond Catholicism, he also saw some of the movement's defects. He regarded the Reformation as resistance to the principle of authoritarianism; but the protest that arose against extreme spiritual despotism of the Roman church was itself rather extreme and somewhat anarchic. That is why Palacký believed that the worldwide historical process that had begun by Protestantism was far from complete. While proclaiming freedom, Protestantism itself led to authoritarianism, particularly under the sway of its two main confessions (Augsburg and Swiss). However, in accordance with its basic principles Protestantism must allow a further development of rational criticism. Above all, it must allow such criticism to cleanse the teaching of Christ of anthropomorphic distortion; Protestant theology has certainly been guilty of anthropomorphism, albeit to a somewhat lesser extent than the Catholic church. Palacký saw no basic difference between admitting one miracle or a hundred thousand miracles. The struggle between Catholicism and Protestantism, as it manifested itself in the Reformation movements of the fifteenth and sixteenth centuries is far from ended, and its fruits will be fully realized only in the course of further evolution.

In the meantime, as long as mankind has not achieved this ultimate state, relatively imperfect Protestantism and Catholicism must come to terms rather than suppress each other. Protestantism deserves credit for improving Catholicism; on the other hand, it has been also guilty of impairing religion. Protestantism and Catholicism need to interact and to exert a mutually beneficial influence.

Palacký was hoping for progress, even though the goal might never be fully realized. Man always exists in two worlds; he longs for the infinite and he soars toward an intuition of the divine, but at the same time he is the slave of matter. Between these two poles there are innumerable degrees, reflecting the subjective needs of various individuals. Both Protestantism and Catholicism have the duty to minister to these needs, and for this reason mutual tolerance—rather than war—should be their watchword. They should compete for beneficent results, since neither the one nor the other is perfect. Palacký saw the contrast between Protestantism and Catholicism as much narrower than that existing between faith and burgeoning atheism, and for this reason time and again he called for tolerance. "Not everyone who is enrolled in the Catholic register and who attends mass is necessarily a true Catholic, nor is everyone who rejects papal authority necessarily a true Protestant. Protestant Jesuits are far from rare and are in every way comparable to the disciples of Loyola."

As we can see, Palacký based his religious philosophy entirely on the principles of free reason. "Religious faith is always intrinsically subjective, and thus never aggressive, no matter what forms it may assume. It becomes aggressive only when it ceases to be an end in itself and becomes perverted into a means for other ends."

As anyone familiar with modern philosophical currents can see, Palacký's religious position is logically derived from the principles of Kantian philosophy. This is evident not only from his terminology and philosophical formulations but from all his historical writing. In particular, Palacký's description of Hussite history reads like a granite epic of the categorical imperative.

In Kantian philosophy Palacký found the natural continuation and philosophic culmination of the Czech Reformation, in particular the ideals of the Brethren. Kant, in his philosophy of religion, placed ultimate emphasis on the moral element rather than on dogmas, ceremonies, or ecclesiastical formalities. Kant insisted on the sovereignty of reason, even in religion. Palacký's philosophical convictions, his universal history, and his Czech history all reflect this spirit, as is evident from the following declaration:

To speak in concrete terms, I must admit that of all the types of Christianity known to me I give preference to the faith of my forefathers, namely that of the Bohemian Brethren—not as it was modified in Herrnhut in the eighteenth century but as it was formed in Bohemia and Moravia during the fifteenth and sixteenth centuries, when it was still more concerned with Christian life than with dogma and when it still clung to the principle of moral improvement through Christian practice. In this the Bohemian Brethren followed the example and the precepts of their first teacher, Jan Hus, who said: "From the very beginning of my study I made it a rule gladly and modestly to abandon my own opinion in any area, whenever I encountered a truer opinion. I did this quite willingly, for those things that we know are negligible compared to those that elude our understanding."

The humanist idea

The second leading idea of Palacký is his humanist idea. As a matter of fact, his humanist idea is firmly founded in his religious beliefs. The Bohemian Brethren movement, being fraternal, was necessarily both religious and humanist. "Only in godliness as an idea," Palacký explained, "does humanity achieve the full expression of its essence." This Kantian formula means that pure humanity is the pinnacle of wisdom and of all human endeavor. This pure humanity requires that man develop fully all of the potentialities for nobility inherent in his own nature. "The real, living, and complete perception of this ideal of humanity is the summit of human wisdom. . . . Pure humanity is the very law of our daily existence. . . . It is the highest and holiest duty of man."

In addition to an echo of the Brethren philosophy, the voice of Kant and Herder can be heard in these statements. With respect to Herder, Palacký said that "the spirit of pure humanity seemed to emanate from him as from its high priest." In the modern era, the humanist ideal has become widely accepted. It is the reigning philosophy of all nations; in the eighteenth century, philosophy and humanism were virtually synonymous. Certainly, modern man has found no better ideal so far. Of course, every nation and every period formulates the contents of this ideal in its own fashion. Just as there are differences among German, English, and French humanism, so the Czech humanist ideal has its own character. The leaders of our modern revival—Kollár, Šafařík, Palacký, Havlíček—have endeavored to define its character.

Palacký attempted to determine the substance of the Czech humanist ideal primarily on the basis of history. From our history he drew the conviction that our nation, in common with all Slavs, was by nature more devout and more peace-loving than our Western neighbors. According to Palacký, the Czech and Slovak nations are humane by natural temperament and character; in fact, they are models of pure humanity. This is why our people strove for reformation and by means of the Reformation created the purest Christian church ever known, the Bohemian Brethren. The Brethren, therefore, constitute a central point in the entire evolution of mankind. The ideal of the Brethren is a milestone in the historical development of the Czech nation and of all mankind. The movement of the Brethren revealed the true nature and humaneness of the Czech people, as well as the people's deep piety. The humaneness of the Brethren is a manifestation of the Czech national spirit, and it is a pinnacle, the center of our history.

These thoughts of Palacký coincide in many respects with Slavophile ideas—the same era led Slavic thinkers to similar conclusions. Of course, there are also significant differences. The Russian Slavophiles derived their national ideal from Orthodoxy and from ancient Russian culture, while Palacký based his stand on the Brethren and Czech culture. In this, he agreed completely with Šafařík and Kollár.

Czech humanism also has some similarity to Polish messianism. The messianists, too, built their ideal on a religious basis—Catholicism—and on Polish history, which resembles ours in many respects. However, Russian Slavophilism is closer to our humanism than Polish messianism.

Both the humanist ideal of Palacký and the ideal of our revival contain two general elements: a religious-moral one and a rational one. Our goal was to strive at the same time for moral edification and rational enlightenment. Our cultural efforts were to be directed toward a harmonious union of character and reason. Palacký, as the director of the society Svatobor (1864), formulated this humanist task quite explicitly, in full accord with his philosophy of history. He identified the qualities that made us excel during the Reformation, and that helped to resuscitate us after our long decline. . . .

(Here follows the same passage quoted on pages 111–13.)

These "true humanist and patriotic endeavors," expounded so forcefully by Palacký, are surely not directed solely to our writers and leaders—the humanist task is the task of our entire nation.

Our reformation and revival

Every thoughtful and conscious Czech must join Palacký in posing to himself the question of whether our reformation was a mere aberration or whether it had real justification and moral significance. This question also implies a related one: what was the moral significance and the justification of the counterreformation?

There is a great gap between the Reformation, which Palacký presents as the pinnacle of our development, and the present era. If the spirit of a nation manifests itself most intimately in religion—and it does—then the discrepancy between our past and our present is painfully clear.

In common with so many others, our nation abandoned polytheism and accepted Christianity; this evolution represented natural progress. From this point of view Palacký saw the Reformation as further evidence of cultural advancement. Palacký rejected the incorrect contention of certain Russian historians that our reformation was merely a continuation of the supposed orthodoxy of Saints Cyril and Methodius.

If our reformation and the emergence of the Bohemian Brethren represented religious, moral, and thus general cultural progress, then the counterreformation must be considered a period of decline, decay. Palacký stated this explicitly, although he placed the blame for our decline not only on the ferocity of the counterreformation but on our own intrinsic moral shortcomings. Unfortunately, Palacký did not give us a history of the Catholic counterreformation; the difficult but urgent task of continuing Palacký's work awaits future historians. This will show the reasons for our decline and the causes of the spiritual failure that facilitated the work of counterreformation forces. We will find that the inadequacies of our reformation were greater and more fatal than admitted by Palacký. Needless to say, this does not imply that the spiritual and physical violence of the counterreformation was justified. Even with all its faults the Reformation movement culminating in the Bohemian Brethren is the summit of our national development; in this Palacký is entirely correct. According to Palacký, our acceptance of the religious principles of the counterreformation represented a decline in our stature as a nation.

The discrepancy between our unremarkable present and our great past was keenly felt by Palacký, as well as by Havlíček, Šafařík, Kollár, and Smetana. All these leaders attempted in various ways to bridge the gap. All of them returned to the fundamental principles of the reformation: taking Catholicization as a given fact, they tried to find a transition from the Protestant past to the Catholic present in the philosophy of humanism. Of course, as spiritual descendants and acknowledged adherents of the Brethren and the Hussites, Kollár, Šafařík, and Palacký defined the humanist ideal totally in the spirit of the Reformation. I do not believe in historical accidents. It was no accident that the three leading pioneers of the revival were Protestants. (Havlíček believed in a Catholicism reformed on the basis of Hussite teaching.) This in itself indicates that the revival was a natural continuation of Reformation ideas.

I said Reformation ideas, rather than Protestant ideas, because the Czech Reformation was fundamentally quite different from German Protestantism—more so than even Palacký realized.

Our revival is not yet completed. It will not be completed until we remove all the desiccated, worn-out formulas and empty official forms from our religion. If we adhere to the principles established by the Brethren, we are sure to reach true piety and humanism.

Palacký hoped that Catholicism and Protestantism would unite in harmonious cooperation and mutual interpenetration. This is possible to some extent, but such a formula is not fully satisfactory. In fact, it is quite insufficient. If, as Palacký recommends, we are to keep faith with the progressive ideas of the Brethren, we cannot merely juggle old elements but we must work toward a new creative synthesis. Palacký himself was driven by his formula to make many a compromise with authoritarianism, a principle that he so eloquently denounced. This matter is so serious that I bring it up in spite of my affection for Palacký and my enormous respect for him—in fact, precisely *because* of that respect. And we certainly owe it to ourselves to admit that one of the main reasons for our flabbiness of character is that unfortunate religious ambiguity, our propensity to pay lip service to both the religion of the past and the religion of the present, while according true loyalty to neither one.

A critical analysis of Palacký's philosophical work of course discloses various details that require reformulation. In particular, today we would no longer hinge the religious and moral problem exclusively on rationality. Ironically, it was precisely the rationalism of Palacký and other awakeners that was so much in tune with the times and therefore so useful for our purposes.

Nor would we place quite as much emphasis nowadays on Kant and German philosophy. But even this allegiance to Kant served a useful role in its time, for our immersion in German philosophy eventually helped us to define our own independent, Czech way of thinking. German philosophy performed the same valuable service for the Russian Slavophiles and the Polish messianists.

If we modify Palacký's philosophical and psychological perspective, our historical development—especially our religious evolution—may appear in a new and more revealing light. Nevertheless, on all the major issues we still can and must follow Palacký, trustfully and cheerfully.

Palacký's doctrines of the state and of nationality

In order to understand Palacký's political aims and tactics we must examine how he understood the state, nationality, and social questions.

According to Palacký, until the year 1848 the state was a centralized entity. Through its centralizing power, which also gave rise to absolutism, the state performed a useful function in organizing a large part of mankind into a single unit. Once this task had been accomplished, however, the time had come for new social and governmental structures. To combat centralism new cultural forces came into being, primarily public opinion and nationalism. Centralism must abdicate in favor of the federation of nations.

Palacký supported this formulation of the goals of the state by pointing to the democratic traditions of our Czech and Slavic ancestors. Palacký contrasted this Slavic conception of the state with the current liberal concept held by the Germans. Palacký repeatedly rejected this brand of liberalism on the ground that it glorified state power over nationality.

Palacký also rejected absolutism and centralism, as well as government by estates. He accepted modern constitutionalism, and he praised the old, democratic Slavic nobility as an example for the Czech aristocracy to emulate.

Palacký believed that the nation and nationality were higher forms of organization than the state. The nation as a unit constituted for Palacký a moral and legal entity. By nationality he understood the consciousness of moral and legal obligations and common awareness of political aspirations. For Palacký, nationality had its full justification in the humanist idea. The humanist concept implies not only the equality of individuals but also of nations as natural entities. The humanist idea, being the foundation and legitimization of the national idea, is intrinsically on a higher plane: "In spite of all my fervent love for my nation, I nevertheless place human and scientific values above national values." In practice, it is not always easy to make such distinctions and to give to nation and humanity their exact due; Palacký, too, erred more than once in this respect.

In his letter to the Frankfurt diet, Palacký cited the progress of humanity and culture in demanding equality between Slav and German. In his manifesto to the Slavic Congress, he invoked the French slogan of liberty, equality, and fraternity for "everybody living in our state," demanding on this basis "complete equality for all nationalities, regardless of size or political power."

Palacký believed that the equality of nations flowed from a natural right and was consistent with humanist demands. "The principle of the equal rights of nations," we read in his *Idea of the Austrian State*, "is just as old as the doctrine of natural law." And in the same work he declared: "The nation with the sum of its spiritual needs and aspirations is just as holy as a human person with his natural rights. . . . The equal right of all to achieve the noblest humanity is God's own law, which none can transgress with impunity."

Nations have a natural right to self-preservation. "After all, they have the duty to educate themselves, that is to kindle and nourish the spark of God in themselves, and no power on earth has the right to absolve them of this obligation. Education of the mind is pure nonsense without education of the tongue, and perfection of language is a precondition for perfection of the spiritual life. Duty is at the same time the mother of right. . . . Thus, having a duty to perfect our language—a duty from which nobody can absolve us—

we also have a corresponding right to do so, and nobody can oppose us or put obstacles in our path. The preservation and perfection of nationality is a moral commandment that cannot be revoked."

In appealing to the ideals of the French Revolution, Palacký maintained that these ideals were consistent with those of ancient Slavic democracy and were simple extensions of the main Christian doctrine. As far as the latter is concerned, Palacký was more correct than he knew, for recent research has confirmed that the doctrine of human rights had its roots in the Reformation.

On the other hand, the concept that the Slavs had a special propensity for democracy requires correction. Here, Palacký indulged in that exaggeration which was typical of all contemporary national philosophies. In spite of his keen critical faculties, Palacký spoke with that Kollár-like Slavic enthusiasm that seized him after the first failures of the constitutional program and that led him to adopt "Slavic cosmopolitanism"—a grandiose idea that Havlíček tried to replace by a truly conscious and carefully thought out Czech Slavicism. Of course, we must not forget what Palacký himself said in 1873, in his well-known answer to Professor Makushev of Warsaw: "If a time ever comes when we must cease being Czechs, then it will be a matter of complete indifference to us whether we become Germans, Italians, Hungarians, or Russians." In the Epilogue, too, where Palacký praised allegiance to Slavic sentiments and mutual devotion between Russians and Czechs, he warned against exaggeration and extravagance, such as the notion that all Slavs should Russify themselves as quickly as possible. He rejected Pan-Russism, as well as the dream of creating a single all-Slavic language. For the same reasons, Palacký frequently attacked plans for the development of literary Slovak, favoring instead a unified Czecho-Slovak language and literature.

By means of his work in history Palacký countered the amorphous, centrifugal Slavic tendencies of the Kollár period with a national idea that was Czech in the true and deep sense of the word. He showed us that in concert with larger and more populous nations, we were called upon to fulfill the highest and noblest tasks. It was not necessary to regard one's own people as the only chosen people; true humanism opposes invidious distinctions of persons, classes, states, cultures, and churches. Nevertheless, Palacký often emphasized national antagonisms—especially between Slavs and Germans—to a greater extent than the need for cooperation and harmony between nations.

Cultural policy of a small nation

Political practice is not merely a logical extension of theoretical principles; it must stand on its own merits. We may therefore recognize the validity of Palacký's historical writings yet have serious doubts about his political tactics. For Palacký, politics was not the same thing as it was for Havlíček. Palacký was naturally more drawn to his historiographic work than to politics. Otherwise he would not have given up political life during the reactionary period, and subsequently he would not have so trustingly delegated political leadership to Clam-Martinic and to Dr. Rieger.

Of course, he had his own reason for his mistrust of politics, and it was an honest one; namely, he believed that the state—and political activity concerned with the state—no longer had the same importance in contemporary life as it did in older times.

This attitude about the state must also be taken into account when examining Palacký's passive political outlook and his conviction that the Czech people could not be politically independent. As indicated earlier, this conviction is one of the fundamental tenets of Palacký's political philosophy. It is like a red thread running through the compilation of his writings in *Radhost*. He stated this opinion for the first time in his solemn message to Frankfurt. The same opinion was expressed in his aphorisms on the state (1848), and in the Manifesto of the National Committee for Uniting Moravia and Silesia with Bohemia (6 May 1848). In his declaration of 21 March 1849, defending the parliamentary policy of the previous two years, Palacký declared that "in view of the centralizing tendencies evident in contemporary life, ideas of national independence for the Hungarians, Czechs, Serbs, Romanians, Ruthenians, and Slovenes, in fact even for the Poles, are nothing but deceptive dreams." He said the same thing in his speech to the Upper House on 27 August 1861, declaring that small states could survive in the Middle Ages but could not exist in the modern era. In the debate about the Polish uprising, he defended this view against the Young Czech party. Palacký's *Idea of the Austrian State* is built around this concept, and the same opinion was echoed in a number of his most important political pronouncements.

Recognizing our small size and limited power, Palacký looked for security in a federation of small Austrian nations. As he said in the aforementioned speech to the Upper House, he believed in associations of nations: "Hungary, just like Bohemia, is driven by fate to join a larger political unit and to submit to the conditions of life in such a larger whole."

As his trip to Moscow demonstrated, Palacký was not deterred from this opinion by the establishment of dualism nor by the supremacy that the Hungarians had arrogated to themselves. Of course, Palacký no longer believed in the omnipotence of the state, whether large or small. He accepted nationalism and public opinion as two forces mightier than the state; he therefore logically stressed the importance of cultural politics, a type of political orientation that we have called "internal."

Palacký particularly stressed the need for national education in 1852. Motivated partly by political considerations, he did not hesitate to demand a popularization of science, especially modern natural science. This viewpoint is all the more remarkable in that in our country the humanist ideas and the national revival have been traditionally identified not with science but with so-called classical, particularly literary, education.

Today conditions are different, not only in our lands but in neighboring countries and in the whole world. We have a university, an academy, and many other institutions that did not exist in Palacký's time. And yet his rousing words are still valid—perhaps they are more necessary now than ever before.

Our national situation has recently deteriorated, and it is constantly deteriorating further. Modern communications, the modern progress of nations in all areas, carefully planned international maneuverings, the relative freedom of action that constitutional government has encouraged, ever mounting industrial and cultural competition, progress in education, journalism, and intellectual communications of all kinds, perfection and broadening of governmental organization—all of these elements are so new and so powerful that they require entirely new formulations of our national program. Let no one be fooled into a false sense of security by our successes. We have had successes, but let us not forget that they must be regarded in relative terms and that we have not progressed to the same degree as other nations, especially the Germans. The outside world does not impinge upon us less forcefully than was true in the time of Kollár or Dobrovský; quite the contrary. If our fathers were satisfied with a Czech word, we must work to turn that word into Czech spirit. Since 1848 and the installation of constitutional government we have been more endangered by Germanization than ever, and the danger is more acute than it was formerly—even in the days of Emperor Joseph II. This statement is not an idle paradox but is based upon careful comparison of our present literature with that of past epochs.

I am not unduly afraid of this situation, but I consider it my duty to point it out. We must turn to the "internal" politics that Palacký urged upon us time and again. Palacký expected salvation only from working for enlightenment.

Needless to say, Palacký did not look upon the program of enlightenment solely in terms of intellectual education, without corresponding attention to character development. Nor did he consider science an end in itself. He explicitly protested against such a viewpoint in his answer to Makushev mentioned earlier; science was to serve the education of men and of nations. He ended his Epilogue on this note, writing:

"My final word consists in the heartfelt and earnest wish that my fellow patriots in Bohemia and Moravia—in whatever circumstances they may find themselves—will never cease to be true to themselves, to truth, and to justice!" And sensing his impending end, Palacký at the threshold of the grave—on 23 April 1876—gave us the following testament: "The time of Hus was a glorious time, the Czech nation then surpassed in spiritual excellence all other nations of Europe. . . . Now, it is necessary for us to educate ourselves and to act according to educated reason. This is the only testament I wish to bequeath to my nation."

In accord with his faith in the progress of humanity, Palacký enthusiastically praised Kant's categorical imperative in his Epilogue. He understood the categorical imperative as "the sense of duty that is the foundation of all human existence. This has shown the way toward everything that is noble and divine in human thought and human aspirations." From this standpoint, Palacký rejected materialism and pantheism, both of which he regarded as sources of enmity between nations and causes of political violence.

It is therefore necessary for the majority of well-meaning people to be active; light must actively fight darkness, right must combat injustice, noble mind must challenge bestial impulse....

With regard to the present mournful situation of our people, I repeat: Let the skies darken over our heads; let the godless—including those kneeling in front of altars and crossing themselves piously—invent ever new and diabolic ways of suppressing, shaming, and tormenting us. I do not appeal for violence to counter violence, knowing that ancient Nemesis is ever near. Rather, I remind, beg—yes, conjure—every good man to throw off indolence, to educate himself, to strive with all his might to strengthen the reign of truth and justice on this earth....

This, in essence, is the program of "the father of our country." It is not only a political program. In an oppressed and dependent nation it is not difficult to articulate political and national demands; the demand for justice and equality is self-evident. The great achievement of Palacký consists in having given these demands a philosophical foundation, grounded in our great historical tradition. This is the reason why a grateful nation acknowledged him as its leader, its father.

In the midst of the current crisis, Palacký's thought should lead us to search our national conscience. Are we acting according to Palacký's Czech idea? Are we furthering this idea?

Palacký showed us that our Czech idea is truly a world idea, an existential question, the most existential of all: it is the idea that the relation of man to man, of nation to nation, must be determined in the most profound possible sense, *sub specie aeternitatis*.

The nation of the Brethren must ever yearn for the infinite. This is the testament of our fathers, and in their spirit it is the testament of the father of our country, František Palacký.

 CHAPTER 6

The Essence
of Political Realism

Havlíček was a forerunner of political realism. . . . He recognized only two kinds of religion: honest and dishonest. In the same way, he recognized only two kinds of politics: rational and irrational.

Nowadays, we would express this attitude by saying that in the last analysis, politics too must conform to objective criteria and must be based on knowledge and morality. The year 1848 marked an important step in that direction on the European continent, as Havlíček well understood.

A political person who thinks in these terms sees the historical development as determined by definite law and order. Such a political analyst studies his era in the same manner that a natural scientist studies nature. We have already remarked that Havlíček saw the laws of nature operating even in history.

Like all precise knowledge, political science as Havlíček envisioned it would be founded on experience. Havlíček always referred to concrete circumstances and realities. This did not mean, however, that Havlíček accepted the contemporary slogan of

From Tomáš G. Masaryk, *Karel Havlíček: Snahy a tužby politického probuzení* (Prague, 1920), pp. 520–22.

"adapting to circumstances"; he explicitly protested against such an attitude. Empiricism is not opportunism.

Nor is political empiricism a blind acceptance of reality. Havlíček constantly called for rationality, he preached rationality even more than experience. In particular, reason was needed to combat wishful thinking and fantastic utopianism. "In politics, we must never give preference to poetic ideas and plans that have no foundation in reality."

For the same reason, Havlíček did not blindly hold to history and to facts given by history; a political realist wants to *make* history.

Political realism believes in progress. Havlíček had faith in evolution; he opposed radicalism and revolution, and—in his words—worked for progress that was peaceful, gradual, permanent, and certain.

Political realism is positive, entirely positive. Radicalism abandons positive progress for adventure on the left, reactionary conservatism for adventure on the right. Both are negative. The radical incites others; the conservative is apathetic. Radical agitation and conservative inertia are opposed by realistic, productive work.

Political realism may appear as the middle road between radicalism and conservatism, but this appearance is deceptive. In fact, realism is continually moving forward, it is not in the middle of two extremes; the two extremes veer off to the sides. Havlíček gave a fitting answer to the political hacks who called for the "golden middle road of the simple, decent Czech man" by pointing out that a dog's tail also follows the common middle road.

When politics is founded on precise observation, on experience illumined by reason, meaningful prediction becomes possible. The radicals substitute malediction and suspicion for prediction. Havlíček put it aptly: "After all, suspiciousness is no proof of clear-sightedness; disbelief is not prophecy."

Radicalism and reaction both represent political dilettantism. The radicals who mock political realists are like quacks ridiculing scientifically trained physicians. Quacks, like radicals, are a species of religious fetishists. Radicals are at best improvisers; reactionaries gain their strength from the weakness of human reason and character.

From the philosophical viewpoint, historical radicalism is materialism. That is its true essence, therefrom derives its faith in violence and its demand for instantaneous victory. Therefrom derives also its revolutionary Romanticism, its glorification of death and violence, its inability to live fully and diligently without excitement and theatricality. Havlíček said: "In the past, men were ready to die for honor and for the good of their people; for these same goals, we are ready to live and to work." These words express the entire meaning of realistic humanism.

Violence, in ever increasing and multiplying ways, is enlarging the realm of physical and spiritual death; our task is to bring this reign to an end.

CHAPTER 7

The Social Question

Through a natural process of evolution, we have progressed from a Kollárian concept of humanism, taken in a one-sided, nationalistic sense, to a broader humanism with a greater social emphasis. I have tried to show that the social question was a central one in all the areas of our thought and work—in politics, literature, art, science, and philosophy. This development followed its natural course until today when the social question is in the very foreground of the Czech question. But the social problem of our nation leads us back to the fifteenth century, for it was then that we first attempted to solve it and we did a poor job. We must now expiate the year 1487. If we fail to find a just solution to social demands, if we do not proceed in the spirit of our historic ideals, in the spirit of universal human ideals, if we turn from love to violence—then we will return to our grave never to be resurrected again.

The social question does not only concern the workers but also morality

The social question is not merely the problem involving workers, just as 1487 was not merely a problem involving peasants. The

From Tomáš G. Masaryk, *Česká otázka: Snahy a tužby národního obrození* (Prague, 1969), Chapter V.

social question is not concerned with a particular class or caste, but it affects all of us. Yielding to the pressure of workers and granting universal suffrage constitutes only a partial and negative approach to the problem; the problem must be solved totally and positively, and this means that heads must become more enlightened, hearts must become warmer; it means that spirit must triumph over matter and narrow self-interest must be transcended.

The social question involves a decision between morality and immorality, between violence and effective humanism.

The social problem is the basis of all our national effort / The task of our socially privileged classes and of the Czech intelligentsia / The progressive movement and labor

Even in the narrower, concrete context of our national politics and partisan strife, the social question plays a prominent part, currently taking the form of the struggle for universal suffrage. We noted earlier that Havlíček had already demanded the universal right to vote, while Palacký mistakenly opposed it. The Young Czech party had long ago made this "democratic" demand a major part of its program. Sladkovský even favored universal representation on a proportional basis. But the matter transcends any particular demand; it concerns the entire social direction of our national strategy. The younger generation understands the task assigned to the socially privileged classes, and Czech students—following the example of their colleagues in other countries—have become active among the workers. The Czech student and the Czech worker are rather close to each other economically and socially. This was already evident in the glowing poems that Rudolf Mayer—the very incarnation of the Czech student—addressed to our working class. Somewhat later, Barák became a lively mediator between students and workers. It is true that these older attempts at contact were more concerned with political and national issues than with social ones, but this was the natural pattern both here and elsewhere. Today it is the social program that is uppermost. But the Czech student or intellectual must not believe that he is the born teacher of the farmer or worker; in many respects he must be their pupil as he still has more to learn than to teach. We must not use labor and other economically or politically submerged classes as means to an end. We would make a serious error if we defined our task with respect to labor only in national or political terms. The task is moral, moral above all else. It is not a question of "winning labor over" to the national cause but of developing a sense for justice throughout our society. The rest will be added unto us.

Social democracy / Herder and Marx / The role of journalism / Limitations of the materialistic outlook / The Czech question and the social question

Organized social democracy is forcing all of us to take our commitment to "the people" seriously. It is true that in opposing universal suffrage the Old Czech party is following the policy of Palacký; however, in this particular instance, loyalty to Palacký is unfortunate. On the other hand, the Young Czechs have not sufficiently clarified their position on political and social reform, and their party is indefinite on specific issues raised by social democracy. Some of their leaders seem to be under the illusion that they have met their obligations simply by supporting the establishment of a national workers' party. Our labor is being accused of a lack of patriotism and of internationalism. However, by joining the international social and democratic organization, our workers are following basically the same route chosen by our intellectuals, writers, and artists; this is quite aside from the fact that capital, too, is organized on an international basis. Furthermore, the evolution of our revival also provides a consistent analogy with the present program of our labor movement. Our workers are just as dependent on German social-democratic ideas as our national awakeners were dependent on German Enlightenment philosophy, and for the same geographic and cultural reasons. What Herder did for our awakeners, Marx has done for our labor leaders.

Working-class journalism and literature are developing under the influence of both German and domestic models. The character of this literature is consistent with traditional prototypes not only in terms of forms but in artistic conception as well. For example, the poems and stories of Krapka are written in a somewhat old-fashioned, romantic genre; new social ideas and plans are fitted into old literary forms. Workers are also reading Pfleger and other older social writers. In accord with the current trend, our revival process has broadened to include ever-widening circles of the people.

These parallels between the organization and evolution of our workers and our bourgeoisie may also be found in the political area. In contrast to the rather centralized organization of German labor, our workers are organized on a more federalistic and autonomous basis. In this respect, too, our workers are revealing their national character; it could not be otherwise, for we are all the sons of the same land and the same period of time, and it behooves us to act like brothers. This has become the core of the current significance of Kollár's humanism.

As far as the reproach of internationalism leveled against the workers is concerned, I have come to the conclusion that our bourgeois class is no more "national" than our labor class—rather less so, in fact. The accusations are baseless. In any case, as long as our writers and journalists continue to ignore the intellectual needs of workers, they have no right to level any reproaches whatever. A poor man barely earning his bread by the sweat of his brow can hardly afford to subscribe to a newspaper costing twenty-five florins or to buy expensive books and magazines. This is quite aside from the content—which is often such as to leave the worker's intellectual hunger unappeased.

With regard to fundamental principles, I have stated several times that I reject the philosophic and sociologic basis of the social democratic program. Socialist philosophy has developed from "classical" philosophy of the eighteenth and nineteenth centuries. This was the origin of the materialistic framework that so-called historical materialism accepted as the philosophical foundation of socialism. In questions dealing with an overall outlook on the world and the ultimate concerns of men, there can, of course, be no compromise. It is not my habit to speak lightly of such matters and to abandon my faith to the mercy of our liberalism and clericalism. I therefore simply repeat that I am decisively opposed to the materialistic view of the world. Nevertheless, I have learned to be tolerant, and I know that a materialist is not necessarily an evil man, nor is an antimaterialist a good one. I have had numerous occasions to observe that the philosophical and theological opponents of materialism are far from admirable persons, when judged by their deeds and lives rather than by their creed and words. If we antimaterialists truly lived in an antimaterialist way, the workers and the social democrats would be forced into the opposite camp.

I therefore make a distinction between the demands and practical political programs of social democracy and its philosophical foundations; I try to differentiate between the justified demands of our downtrodden labor and the alien philosophy that was foisted upon it by our unjust society and our apathy.

On the whole, I find the specific political and social demands made by our workers to be justified, and I have always felt a moral duty to support these demands with all the means at my command. I am not an expert in economics, and I hesitate to make definite statements in this area. However, I think I can say that the critique made by Marx and other socialist thinkers is justified and generally correct, although the underlying theoretical concepts have no greater intrinsic value than other honest, carefully elaborated theories.

I can understand why social democrats have turned Marx into an untouchable authority, but I am not pleased by this attitude. In any case, I know perfectly well that I have no reason or right to oppose demands for justice or equality, no matter from whom such demands may come or from what principle they originate. "Or what man is there of you, whom if his son ask bread, will he give him a stone?" And stones are exactly what we are giving our workers day by day—literary, philosophical, theological, political stones.

Since I see the solution to the social question primarily in terms of moral regeneration, I do not share the view that has been adopted in this matter by the clerical party, although I concede that the clerical concept in this case is superior to that adopted by the liberals. Our clerical leaders, too, have understood the significance of the social question and they have surpassed both the Old Czechs and Young Czechs in this regard. Under the stimulus of a perceptive political leader on the papal throne, Czech Catholics are beginning to follow the road taken by progressive Catholicism in Germany and France.

If we are to fulfill the ideals of our ancestors and national awakeners, the ideals of universal world humanism so indefatigably proclaimed by Kollár, all segments of our nation must join in dedicated effort. Our aristocracy, in particular, has a great duty to perform; it is surely unnecessary to point out that it is our aristocracy, above all, who must expiate the year 1487.

But we must not wait for our nobles to take the lead. We all have our tasks to perform, new and old, duties continually growing in scope and number. We must begin at once to help answer the Czech question, and we must continue to answer it—individually and as a nation—every day anew.

Biographical Index

Anton, Karl Gottlob (1751–1818): 62, 70–72
Anton was a lawyer, historian, and ethnographer who devoted himself to Lusatian studies. He corresponded with many Slavic scholars including Dobrovský and Pelcl. His main work is *Erste Linien eines Versuches über der alten Slaven-Ursprung, Sitten, Gebräuche, Meinungen und Kenntnisse* (I, 1783; II, 1789).

Bach, Alexander (1813–84): 96
Bach was an Austrian lawyer and statesman. He was responsible for bureaucratic and social reforms during Emperor Franz Joseph's reign. At first a political liberal, Bach later became a conservative when he was appointed to Prince Schwarzenberg's cabinet as minister of justice (1848–49) and then as minister of the interior (1849–59). He was removed from the cabinet in 1859 as a result of mounting discontent on the part of the populace.

Barák, Josef (1833–83): 120, 144
Barák was a Czech writer, translator, publicist, and newspaper editor. He was very active in arousing nationalist feelings among his people and was imprisoned on several occasions. He published the democratic weekly *Svoboda* (*Freedom*) from 1867 to 1873; he was editor-in-chief of *Národní listy* (*The National Paper*) from 1874 until his death.

Batyushkov, Konstantin Nikolayevich (1787–1855): 50
Batyushkov, a leading Russian poet of the early nineteenth century, was one of Pushkin's precursors.

Bayer, Gottlieb Siegfried (1694–1738): 43
Bayer, a German scholar, obtained the chair of eastern antiquities

and languages at the Russian Academy of Sciences in 1725. He also participated in the founding of the Academy gymnasium. Bayer was the founder of the "Scandinavian School" in Russian historiography.

Bestuzhev-Ryumin, Konstantin Nikolayevich (1829–97): 43
Bestuzhev-Ryumin was professor of Russian history at St. Petersburg University and a member of the Academy. His views represent late Slavophilism. He believed that a historian's task was to study "national consciousness." He wrote numerous articles and *Russian History* (2 vols., 1872–85).

Blahoslav, Jan (1523–1571): 4
Blahoslav was a Czech humanist and the foremost writer of the Brethren in the sixteenth century. He became bishop of the Brethren and contributed eight volumes to their history. His translation of the New Testament (1564) into the vernacular was incorporated into the great Kralická Bible (1588).

Bolzano, Bernard (1781–1848): 18, 47, 78, 91, 107
Bolzano was a philosopher, mathematician, and theologian. A priest, he became professor of philosophy and theology at the University of Prague in 1805. He was elected secretary of the Bohemian Academy of Sciences in 1841. Bolzano was one of the most important logicians of the nineteenth century; his religious philosophy belongs to the tradition of Josephinism.

Boniface VIII (c. 1235–1303): 27
Boniface VIII (Benedetto Gaetano) was the pope (1294–1303) who issued the famous bull *Unam sanctam* (1302) asserting the supremacy of the spiritual power over the temporal.

Brodziński, Kazimierz (1791–1835): 56
Brodziński was a prominent Polish writer and poet. He has been called precursor of Adam Mickiewicz because of his rejection of pseudo-Classicism and his efforts to regenerate Polish poetry on a national basis under the banner of Romanticism.

Budilovich, Anton Semyonovich (1846–1908): 52
Budilovich was a Russian Slavist who ardently supported the idea of Slavic unity. He was active as a linguist, literary historian, and publicist.

Byron, George Gordon (1788–1824): 25

Cabet, Étienne (1788–1856): 82
Cabet was a French Socialist whose ideas were influenced by Sir Thomas More and Robert Owen. He was exiled in 1834 for criticizing the government. During 1848–49 he led a group of his followers to the United States and they founded a settlement at Nauvoo, Illinois.

Catherine II (the Great), Empress of Russia (1762–96): 32, 34

Čelakovský, František Ladislav (1799–1852): 19, 42, 47, 50, 53, 56, 84
   Čelakovský was a Czech poet, translator, and scholar with a special interest in folklore (inspired by Herder's ideas). He published his three-volume *Slovanské národní písně* (*Slavic Folk Songs*) in 1822–27. Later he published his own creative adaptations of Slavic folk songs: *Ohlas písní ruských* (*The Echo of Russian Songs*, 1829) and *Ohlas písní českých* (*The Echo of Czech Songs*, 1839). Čelakovský also produced a collection of Slavic proverbs, *Mudrosloví národa slovanského v příslovích* (*The Wisdom of the Slavic Nation in Proverbs*).

Čermák, Jaroslav (1831–78): 106
   Čermák was a Czech painter whose works won him several awards abroad. He dealt mainly with historical themes relating to the Czech past and with southern Slav subjects.

Chaadayev, Petr Yakovlevich (1794–1856): 50
   Chaadayev was a brilliant Russian liberal who became a convert to mystical Catholicism. He arrived at an extremely negative view of Russian history and sharply criticized Russia in his *Philosophical Letters*. When the first of these was published in *The Telescope* in 1836, the magazine was suppressed, and the author was officially declared to be insane.

Chalupka, Samo (1812–83): 53
   Chalupka was an outstanding Slovak poet who took part in the Polish insurrection of 1830–31.

Charlemagne, Emperor of the West (800–814): 39

Charles IV, King of Bohemia (1346–78) and Holy Roman Emperor (1355–78): 5, 10, 21, 123

Chelčický, Petr (c. 1390–1460): 4, 6, 8, 10–11, 13, 89
   Chelčický, like Jan Hus, was a great religious thinker who contributed to the Czech Reformation. He was both a primitive Christian anarchist and a pacifist; his ideas were inspired by Wycliffe, Hus, Štítný, etc. His masterpiece is *Sít' víry* (*The Net of Faith*).

Clam-Martinic, Jindřich Jaroslav, Count (1826–87): 87–88, 136
   Clam-Martinic, a member of the feudal nobility, was active in Bohemian politics and gave support to the Old Czech party of Palacký and Rieger.

Comte, Auguste (1798–1857): 73
   Comte was a French philosopher and sociologist who founded the doctrine of positivism. His major work is *Cours de philosophie positive* (6 vols., 1830–42).

Cyril (Constantine), St. (826 or 827–69): 10, 96–97, 131
   Constantine-Cyril and his brother Methodius headed a Byzantine

cultural mission to Moravia in 863. Constantine-Cyril invented a special alphabet—Glagolitic—in order to translate the Holy Scriptures and liturgical books into Slavic. The result of the mission was the founding of a new Slavic church and the beginning of Slavic literature.

Danilov, Ivan (1817–19): 59
A Cossack and Kollár's teacher of Russian in Jena.

Dobner, Job Felix Gelasius (1719–90): 21, 34
Dobner was the most famous Czech historian of the eighteenth century. He has been designated the "father" of Czech critical history.

Dobrovský, Josef (1753–1829): 17, 19–23, 25, 28, 34–35, 36–45, 46, 47–48, 50, 51–52, 54, 56, 58, 79, 110, 124, 138
Dobrovský, the "father" of comparative Slavic studies, was the greatest scholar of the Czech Enlightenment. His work spanned many fields including history, literature, philology, and folklore. Writing in Latin or German, he published, among other works, practical grammars, a Czech-German dictionary, and a history of Czech literature.

Dostoevsky, Fyodor Mikhaylovich (1821–81): 64, 66, 69

Durych, Václav (1735–1802): 21, 34
Durych, a priest, was the first Czech Slavist. Among other things he was responsible for interesting Dobrovský in Slavic studies.

Eötvös, József, Baron (1813–71): 80
Eötvös was a Hungarian writer and politician whose liberal views led him to work for social and political reforms.

Erben, Karel Jaromír (1811–70): 84
Erben was the second great Czech Romantic poet (the first being Mácha). He was a man of many talents. His original poetic output was small and consists primarily of a collection of ballads, *Kytice z pověstí národních* (*A Bouquet of Folktales*, 1853). He also collected Slavic and Czech folk songs and tales (e.g., *Písně národní v Čechách* [*Folk Songs in Bohemia*], 1841), published old texts, did research in archives, wrote articles for Rieger's encyclopedia on the Slavic folk epos and translated several important works from Russian literature (e.g., *The Igor Tale*).

Ewers, Johann Philipp (1781–1830): 43
Ewers was a Russo-German historian who became a professor at Yuryev (Dorpat) University. While engaged in his study of Russian history, he was in constant contact with Karamzin.

Filangieri, Gaetano (1752–88): 32, 34
Filangieri was an Italian jurist of liberal principles who devoted himself to the study of law. He presented an ideal conception of modern legislation in his unfinished but widely translated *La Scienza della legislazione* (8 vols., 1781–88).

Frederick II, King of Prussia (1740–86): 33, 44

Fries, Jacob Friedrich (1773–1843): 16, 17, 22, 57
Fries was a German philosopher and mathematician who held professorships at Jena and Heidelberg. He was influenced by Kant and Friedrich Heinrich Jacobi.

Gaj, Ljudevit (1809–72): 28
Gaj, a Croatian, was a prominent awakener of his people and the creator of Illyrianism, a concept indicating the totality of the South Slavic lands (with the exception of Bulgaria). He exerted his influence through a political newspaper that he started in 1834.

Galileo Galilei (1564–1642): 113

Garshin, Vsevolod Mikhaylovich (1855–88): 66
Garshin was a Russian prose writer whose works are characterized by the compassion of a "conscience-stricken nobleman" for the people.

Goethe, Johann Wolfgang (1749–1832): 44, 64

Gogol, Nikolay Vasilyevich (1809–52): 50, 66
Russian novelist and dramatist, whose *Dead Souls* and *The Inspector General* are world famous.

Griboyedov, Aleksandr Sergeyevich (1795–1829): 50
Griboyedov was a playwright and poet whose masterpiece *Woe from Wit* is one of the greatest Russian comedies.

Gurowski, Adam (1805–66): 53
Gurowski was a Polish publicist. He participated in the insurrection of 1830–31 and then went to Paris. His original anti-Russian feelings underwent a total conversion, and he began to propagate a Pan-Slavism in which Russia held the central position. Tsar Nicholas allowed him to return to Russia, but he soon left for Germany.

Hálek, Vítězslav (1835–74): 86, 101–5, 120
Hálek was a Czech poet and critic. He was one of the Májovci, a group of democratic and socially conscious writers centered around the almanac *Máj*.

Hanka, Václav (1791–1867): 19, 41, 47, 51–52, 54
Hanka was a student of Dobrovský and a follower of Kopitar. He wrote lyric poetry, translated from other Slavic languages, edited Old Czech texts, and published grammars of Czech, Old Church Slavic, Russian, and Polish. He was probably the chief forger of the *Rukopis Královédvorský* and the *Rukopis Zelenohorský*, two manuscripts of alleged early origin.

Harms, Friedrich (1819–80): 22
Harms was a German professor of philosophy at Kiel, Jena, and Berlin.

Havlíček (-Borovský), Karel (1821–56): 14, 18, 58, 76–83, 85–88, 90–91, 92, 94–96, 97, 99–102, 105, 107, 110, 111, 113–15, 119–20, 124, 129, 132, 135–36, 140–41, 144

Havlíček was a leading Czech political figure, editor, critic, and writer. After spending two years (1843–44) in Russia as a tutor, he returned home. His initial enthusiasm for that country gave way to a critical attitude toward Russian absolutism and its institutions, as can be seen from his *Obrazy z Rus* (*Pictures from Russia*, 1843–46). Havlíček edited various Czech publications from 1846 to 1851: *Pražské noviny* (*Prague News*), *Česká včela* (*The Czech Bee*), *Národní noviny* (*National News*), and *Slovan* (*Slav*). During this period he tried to develop literary criticism on the basis of Lessing's theories (cf., his *Kapitoly o kritice*, 1846) and led the fight for Czech freedom. He was finally deported to the Tyrol in 1851. Havlíček's greatest literary work was *Křest svatého Vladimíra* (*The Baptism of Saint Vladimir*, published 1876), an unfinished satirical poem on the Christianization of Russia which actually attacks the contemporary Austrian state and its institutions.

Hegel, Georg Wilhelm Friedrich (1770–1831): 18, 25, 74, 107–8
German philosopher.

Herbart, Johann Friedrich (1776–1841): 18, 107
Herbart was an important German philosopher who founded a system encompassing logic, metaphysics, psychology, and aesthetics. He taught at Göttingen and Königsberg.

Herder, Johann Gottfried (1744–1803): 15, 17–18, 22, 25, 28–30, 32–34, 36, 37–38, 47–48, 50, 56, 58, 60–62, 66, 70–71, 72–74, 75, 83–85, 102, 129, 145–46
German critic, poet, and philosopher of history.

Herzen, Alexander (1812–70): 66
Russian writer and revolutionary. His memoirs, *My Past and Thoughts* (1852–55) are his most famous work.

Hoefler, Konstantin (1811–97): 124–25
Hoefler was a German historian with strong clerical views who taught at Munich and Prague (1851–81). He published some Glagolitic fragments with Šafařík in 1857. His edited *Die Geschichtsschreiber der hussitischen Bewegung* (2 vols., 1865–66), which was severely criticized by Palacký.

Hume, David (1711–76): 36, 84
Scottish philosopher.

Hus, Jan (c. 1374–1415): 1–6, 10–11, 12–13, 14, 69–70, 89, 91, 124, 129, 138
Czech reformer who was burned at the stake in 1415.

Hyna, Karel Ferdinand (1802–81): 21
Hyna, a priest, was a Czech philosopher and pedagogue. His most

important work was the two-volume *Dušeslоví zkušebné* (*Experimental Psychology*).

Jelačić (of Bužim), Josef (1801–59): 95
Jelačić was a popular Croatian officer whom the local nationalists elected as governor (*bán*) of a proposed single triune kingdom consisting of Croatia, Slavonia, and Dalmatia in 1848. The Emperor, however, appointed Jelačić governor of Croatia alone and honored him with promotion to general. Although he retained his political office, Jelačić was ultimately unsuccessful in his efforts to further the cause of the southern Slavs.

Jeroným (of Prague) (c. 1380–1416): 12
Jeroným of Prague was a friend and collaborator of Jan Hus. He was a philosopher and politician rather than a theologian. In 1399 he traveled to England where he studied Wycliffe's works, which he later took back to Prague. After defending Wycliffe's doctrine in debates in Paris and Heidelberg, Jeroným returned to Prague in 1407. An eloquent speaker, he was instrumental in obtaining the decree of Kutná Hora from King Wenceslaus IV two years later. This abolished the foreigners' privileged position at the University of Prague. Jeroným pledged to support Hus at the Council of Constance and was later arrested, tried, and sentenced to death at the stake.

Joseph II, Holy Roman Emperor (1765–90): 7, 10, 20, 55, 124, 138

Jungmann, Josef (1773–1847): 19, 36, 37, 40–41, 44, 46–47, 49–53, 54–56, 89–90, 102, 116
Jungmann was a Czech nationalist scholar, writer, and translator. He knew many languages and translated widely from the literatures of various countries, schools, and periods. Most influential were his translations of Chateaubriand's *Atala* and Milton's *Paradise Lost*. He wrote *Slovesnost* (*Literature*), a handbook of literary forms and devices; *O jazyku českém* (*On the Czech Language*), a defense of the Czech language and literature; and a *History of Czech Literature* (1825). His greatest achievement, however, was his Czech-German dictionary in five volumes (1835–39).

Kamarýt, František Dobromil (1812–72): 91
Kamarýt was a Czech religious writer. He prepared a volume of "rhymed maxims" for print in 1867, but it was not published until 1897.

Kampelík, František Cyrill (1805–72): 41, 57
Kampelík was a Czech doctor and writer whose ardent patriotism led Kollár to dedicate one of the sonnets in *Slávy dcera* to him.

Kant, Immanuel (1724–1804): 18, 25, 87–88, 107, 128–29, 133, 138
German philosopher.

Karamzin, Nikolay Mikhaylovich (1766–1826): 56, 60, 62
Karamzin was an important Russian writer and historian who was a

literary liberal but a political conservative. In literature he carried out crucial reforms of the language and headed the Sentimental School in Russia. His *History of the Russian State* (11 vols., 1816–18; vol. 12, unfinished, published posthumously) justified the autocracy.

Kheraskov, Mikhail Matveyevich (1733–1807): 35
Kheraskov was a Russian poet who wrote two long narrative works on national themes in an effort to give his country an epic. He also served as curator of Moscow University.

Khomyakov, Aleksey Stepanovich (1804–60): 28, 57
Khomyakov was a Russian poet, philosopher of history and theologian. He was one of the creators of Slavophilism.

Kiesewetter, Johann Gottfried (1766–1819): 50
Kiesewetter was a German philosopher, one of the most ardent adherents of Kantian philosophy.

Kireyevsky, Ivan (1806–56): 26–28, 50, 66
Kireyevsky was a Russian philosopher, journalist, and editor who became one of the leading Slavophiles.

Klácel, František (1808–82): 21, 47, 91
Klácel was a Czech priest who was active as a philosopher, writer, and newspaper editor. He was persecuted for his free-thinking based on Hegelian philosophy and for his association with Czech patriots and Pan-Slavists. He ended his unhappy life in America.

Klopstock, Friedrich Gottlieb (1724–1803): 50
Klopstock was a German poet whose *Der Messias*, an epic in hexameters, had a tremendous impact on the literature of his country. He also wrote lyric poetry, odes, dramas, and some prose.

Knobloch, František (1746–1804): 42
Knobloch was a patriotic Czech priest. Dlabač addressed a poem to him in 1782.

Kohl, Johann Peter (1698–1778): 43
Kohl was a German scholar who was appointed to the chair of rhetoric and church history at the Imperial Academy of Sciences in St. Petersburg in 1725. He remained in Russia only two years, but he made significant contributions to the study of Russian church history and literature.

Kollár, Jan (1793–1852): 13–23, 25–33, 36–37, 40–42, 43, 45, 46–60, 62, 66–67, 73–75, 79, 80, 82–84, 89, 94–96, 99–100, 101–2, 105, 107–8, 110–11, 113–18, 124, 129–30, 132, 135, 139, 146, 148
Kollár, a Slovak Protestant clergyman, was a poet and a scholar. His *Slávy dcera* (*Slava's Daughter*, 1824; 2nd ed., 1832), a sonnet cycle combining the themes of love and Pan-Slavism, reflected the Romantic ideology of his time. This work had a considerable influence upon

Czech and Slovak literature. In 1849 Kollár became professor of Slavic antiquities at Vienna.

Komenský (Comenius), Jan Amos (1592–1670): 4, 6, 8, 10–11, 13, 21, 89, 109–10, 116–17, 118
Komenský (Comenius) was a great Czech humanist, writer, and thinker. He was ordained in 1616 and later served as the last bishop of the Czech Brethren. After 1620 he lived most of his life in exile. He died in Holland. His greatest literary work was *Labyrint světa a ráj srdce* (*The Labyrinth of the World and the Paradise of the Heart*, 1623), an allegory on the vanity of life in this world. Komenský was the first modern philosopher of education. In 1657 he published his *Didactica magna*, which deals with the education of youth. Although he was offered the presidency of Harvard College, Komenský did not accept the position.

Kopitar, Jernej (1780–1844): 28, 37–38, 43, 57
Kopitar was an outstanding Slovene philologist and Slavist. His grammar of the Slovene language (*Ljubljana*, 1808) had a significance comparable to that of Dobrovský's grammatical works. In 1808 Kopitar went to Vienna where he obtained a position at the court library. Among his other scholarly writings, his second book, an edition (with sources and translations) of two important Slavic monuments (the *Glagolita clozianus* and the tenth-century *Frisian Fragments*), is especially noteworthy. Also significant is his voluminous correspondence with such scholars as Dobrovský and Šafařík.

Kościusko, Tadeusz Andrzéj (1746–1817): 27
Kosciusko was a Polish officer and statesman who won fame as a revolutionary. He was both a leader of the Polish insurrection of 1794 and a participant in the American Revolutionary War.

Král, Josef (1853–1917): 44
Král was a leading Czech classical philologist.

Krapka, Josef (pseud. Náchodský) (1862–1909): 145–46
Krapka was a socialist writer and organizer. In 1907 he attended a meeting of the Second International at Stuttgart and met Lenin.

Krasiński, Zygmunt (1812–59): 50
Krasiński was a Polish poet of distinction. Together with Mickiewicz and J. Slowacki he contributed to the flowering of his nation's poetry in the first half of the nineteenth century.

Křišťan of Prachatice (after 1360–1439): 4
Křišťan of Prachatice was a learned Czech theologian, mathematician, astronomer, and doctor. He was among the first to be influenced by Wycliffe's writings, and Hus considered him to be his teacher. His activity ceased with Hus's death.

Krug, Wilhelm Trautgott (1770–1842): 50
Krug was a German philosopher who taught at Frankfurt-on-Oder, Königsberg, and Leipzig. In 1834 he gave up his chair at Leipzig but remained active as a publicist and a scholar.

Krylov, Ivan Andreyevich (1769–1844): 50
Krylov was a Russian poet, playwright, and satirical journalist. His *Fables* were his masterpiece.

Leonhardi, Hermann Karl (1809–75): 107
Leonhardi was a German philosopher who held a professorship at the University of Prague. He was the leading representative of Krause's philosophy in Bohemia.

Leopold II, Holy Roman Emperor (1790–92): 38–39

Lermontov, Mikhail Yurevich (1814–41): 50
Lermontov was a major Russian lyric poet and prose writer and a leading representative of Romanticism.

Leroy-Beaulieu, Henri Jean-Baptiste Anatole (1842–1912): 65–66, 67
Leroy-Beaulieu was a French historian and publicist. He spent nine years (1872–81) in Russia and then became professor of modern history at the École Libre des Sciences Politiques in Paris. Originally he had been engaged in the study of art and its history, but his stay in Russia turned his attention elsewhere. His major work was *L'Empire des Tsars et les Russes* (3 vols., 1882–89).

Loquis, Martin: 4
Loquis (Latin nickname of Martin Houska) was a Taborite priest (a Pickhart) executed at the behest of Žižka in 1421.

Louis XIV, King of France (1643–1715): 29

Loyola, Ignatius (1491–1556): 128

Luden, Heinrich (1780–1847): 57, 84
Luden was a German historian who taught at Jena. He belonged to a school that was influenced by the liberal and humanitarian ideas of the time.

Luther, Martin (1483–1546): 10, 69–70

Mácha, Karel Hynek (1810–36): 25, 101–2
Mácha was the greatest Czech Romantic and perhaps the greatest Czech poet of all time. He was not fully appreciated until the twentieth century. In his masterpiece *Máj* (*May*, 1836), a narrative poem, Mácha displayed a brilliant command of verse technique.

Maksimovich, Mikhail Aleksandrovich (1804–73): 56
Maksimovich was an outstanding Ukrainian scholar who was active

in the natural sciences, philology, historiography, and ethnography. Among his many publications were several collections of Ukrainian folk songs.

Makushev, Vikenty Vasilyovich (1837–83): 135, 138,
Makushev was a Russian Slavic scholar who wrote extensively on the southern Slavs and from 1871 was a professor at the University of Warsaw.

Malý, Jakub Josef (1811–85): 53–54, 102
Malý was a patriotic Czech writer and editor. A very prolific and many-sided writer, he produced works of uneven quality.

Mánes, Josef (1820–71): 106
Mánes was a talented Czech painter noted for his works on historical and patriotic themes. He was one of the founders of the Jednota Vytvarných Umělcův (Union of Graphic Artists) in 1849.

Marek, Antonín (1785–1877): 19, 21, 36, 47, 49–50, 52–53, 54–55, 116
Marek was a Czech clergyman, writer, and awakener. He met Jungmann in 1804, and they became lifelong friends. His poems and philosophical writings are his most important works. His two verse epistles to Jungmann made him famous; the first "Marek Jungmannovi" ("Marek to Jungmann," published 1814) was a bold political poem. In both he shows himself to be a forerunner of Kollár. Marek also translated poetry from foreign languages with great success. As a philosophical writer he produced a *Logic* and a *Metaphysics.*

Maria Theresa, Queen of Hungary and Bohemia (1740–80): 124

Marx, Karl (1818–83): 145, 147

Matěj of Janov (c. 1350–94): 4, 12
Matěj of Janov was a Czech priest and one of Hus's predecessors. He studied theology for six years in Paris and later was a student of Milíč of Kroměříž. His significance lies primarily in his emphasis on the study of the Bible. He provided a basis and support for the reform movement with his theological erudition.

Mauritius, Flavius Tiberius (c. 539–602): 66
Mauritius was a Byzantine Emperor (582–602) whose armies fought campaigns against the Avars and the Slavs.

Mayer, Rudolf (1837–65): 104, 144
Mayer was an oustanding Czech poet and one of the leading members of the Májovci (a group centered around the almanac *Máj*).

Methodius, St. (c. 815–84): 9–10, 96–97, 131. *See* entry for Cyril (Constantine), St.

Metlinsky, Amvrosy Lukyanovich (1814–70): 56
Metlinsky was a Ukrainian poet and scholar who was interested in folklore. He published a collection of folk songs (1854) that remained an important contribution to the subject for many years.

Mickiewicz, Adam (1798–1855): 25–28, 50, 53
Mickiewicz was a great Polish poet and patriot whose stature is comparable to Pushkin's in Russia. The initiator of Polish Romanticism, Mickiewicz wrote almost no poetry after 1834 when he published his great epic *Pan Tadeusz*. In 1840 he was appointed the first professor of Slavic literature at the Collège de France.

Mikuláš of Pelhřimov (?-c. 1459): 4, 12
Mikuláš of Pelhřimov stood with the radical Hussite faction at the beginning of the Czech religious movement. He became bishop of the Taborites in 1420 and represented their doctrine in numerous conflicts with the Prague masters. With the fall of Tábor in 1452 Mikuláš was imprisoned; he spent the rest of his life in captivity.

Milíč of Kroměříž, Jan (?-1374): 4
Milíč of Kroměříž was an outstanding representative of Czech religious life. Along with Konrad of Waldhausen and Matěj of Janov he was an important forerunner of Hus. He provided an example of a mystically pious life; in his passionate love of poverty he resembled Francis of Assisi. An eloquent preacher for church reform, he was also the founder of an entire school of pulpit eloquence.

Milton, John (1608–74): 19

Montesquieu, Baron de La Brède et de (1689–1755): 47
Author of *De l'Esprit des lois*, French writer, and sociologist.

Müller, Gerhard Friedrich (1705–83): 43
Müller was a German historian who studied in Russia at the Imperial Academy of Sciences. In 1731 he was appointed professor, and in the following year he began to issue an anthology called *Sammlung Russischer Geschichte* (9 vols., 1732–65). This was the first scholarly effort to acquaint foreigners with Russia and her history.

Nadezhdin, Nikolay Ivanovich (1804–1856): 56
Nadezhdin was a many-sided Russian scholar and critic. As a student he became acquainted with German philosophy from which he derived his view of history. He wrote his dissertation on Romantic poetry (1830). In 1831 he founded the magazine *The Telescope*; it was suppressed five years later (cf., Chaadayev), and Nadezhdin was banished from Moscow. His activity as a critic and publicist thus ended.

Náhlovský, František (1807–53): 91
Náhlovský was a Czech clergyman and reformer. He studied philosophy at Prague and theology at Litoměřice where he was ordained in

1830. He took part in the political movement of 1848 as a member of the Národní Výbor (National Committee).

Napoleon I, Emperor of France (1770–1821): 24–25, 27, 28

Neděle, Filip (1778–1825): 91
Neděle was a Moravian priest and religious writer. In 1806 he became professor of biblical studies at the Brno Theological Institute. He was removed from his teaching position in 1820 after a disagreement with the bishop.

Němcová, Božena (1820–62): 104
Němcová was a major Czech prose writer who introduced new forms (the village story and novel) and developed a style suitable for them. Like Erben, Němcová was interested in ethnography, and she contributed two important collections of folktales: *Národní báchorky a pověsti* (*Folk Stories and Tales*, 1845–47) and *Slovenské pohádky a pověsti* (*Slovak Stories and Tales*, 1857–58). In the middle 1840s she started to write tales of peasant life based on the materials that she was collecting. Her masterpiece *Babička* (*Grandmother*), a novel of village life incorporating her own childhood memories, was published in 1855.

Neruda, Jan (1834–91): 104–5, 120
Neruda was a major Czech journalist, poet, and prose writer. His feuilletons and newspaper articles made a great contribution to the development of the modern Czech journalistic style. As a lyric poet he published many collections of verse such as *Hřbitovní kvítí* (*Cemetery Flowers*, 1857), *Písně kosmické* (*Cosmic Songs*, 1878) and *Zpěvy páteční* (*Good Friday Songs*, 1896), Neruda was more original as a prose writer, however; his *Malostranské povídky* (1878), a collection of stories about life in the old Malá Strana section of Prague, is a masterpiece and one of the classics of Czech prose.

Nicholas I, Emperor of Russia (1825–55): 54

Oken, Lorenz (1779–1851): 57
Oken was a German doctor and philosopher. He was professor of medicine at Jena, Munich, and Zurich. As a philosopher he published *Lehrbuch der Naturphilosophie* (3rd ed., 1843) and *Lehrbuch der Naturgeschichte* (3 vols., 1813–27).

Palacký, František (1779–1876): 8, 13–14, 18–19, 22, 25, 41–42, 44, 46, 47, 51, 56, 58, 78–83, 85–88, 90, 91–92, 94–96, 97–99, 107, 110–11, 113–17, 118–20, 122–39, 144–145
Palacký, the "father" of Czech historiography, was a great scholar and statesman. He was influenced by Jungmann and Dobrovský with whom he studied history. Along with Šafařík he published *Počátkové českého básnictví* (*The Beginnings of Czech Poetry*) in 1818. He founded and

edited (1827–38) *Časopis českého musea* (*Journal of the Czech Museum*); he conceived the idea of Matice Česká (founded 1831), a patriotic organization designed for publishing scholarly works in Czech and for supporting the Czech language and literature. Having carefully studied a huge number of sources, Palacký wrote and published a history of Bohemia, at first in German (*Geschichte von Böhmen*, 1836–67) and later in Czech (*Dějiny národu českého v Čechách a v Moravě*, 1848–75). As a political figure he was active from 1848 when he became the leader of the Czech delegation to the Austrian parliament and presided over the Pan-Slavic Congress at Prague. Until his death he remained the major political leader of his people. His Old Czech party favored the so-called Austro-Slavic position.

Palkovič, Jiří (1769–1850): 47
Palkovič was a professor of Czechoslovak language and literature at Bratislava (Pressburg), a writer, and a publisher.

Pelcl, František Martin (1734–1801): 34
Pelcl was a Czech awakener and historian. He was named professor of Czech at Prague University in 1793. His major works were *Kaiser Karl der Vierte, König in Böhmen* (2 vols., 1780–81) and *Lebensgeschichte des römischen und böhmischen König Wenzeslaus* (2 vols. 1788–90).

Peter I (the Great), Emperor of Russia (1689–1725): 32

Pfleger-Moravský, Gustav (1833–75): 104, 146
Pfleger-Moravský was a Czech poet, novelist, and playwright. He achieved literary importance as a novelist. His masterpiece is *Z malého světa* (*From the Small World*, 1863), especially noteworthy for the power of its realistic details and its treatment of social relations between workers and their employers.

Pogodin, Mikhail Petrovich (1800–75): 28
Pogodin was a leading Moscow journalist and a professor of Russian history. He was editor of several magazines and occupied a central position in Moscow literary life for half a century.

Procopius (sixth century A.D.): 66
Procopius was a Byzantine historian. His works constitute a valuable source for the study of the first half of the sixth century.

Proudhon, Pierre Joseph (1809–65): 82
Proudhon was a French social reformer who wrote prolifically on monetary, economic, and political matters. Karl Marx attacked his program for economic reform in 1847.

Puchmajer, Antonín Jaroslav (1769–1820): 17, 19, 21, 23, 34–35, 38, 40, 47, 51–52

Puchmajer was a Czech priest, poet, and scholar. He wrote religious and patriotic verse, idylls, fables, and lyrics. He is considered to be the first modern Czech poet of any real merit. As a scholar (he studied with Dobrovský) he wrote books on economics, a Russian grammar, and a Czech-Russian spelling book. He also assisted Dobrovský with the dictionary.

Purkyně, Jan Evangelista (1787–1869): 114, 116
Purkyně was a famous Czech physiologist who did pioneering work in experimental psychology, histology, and embryology. He became professor of physiology at Breslau University in 1823; twenty-seven years later he was appointed professor at the University of Prague. Purkyně also played an active role in the Czech national movement. He published numerous articles on Czech and Slovak literature in German periodicals, translated Schiller's poetry and Tasso's *Gerusalemme liberata* into Czech, took part in the Pan-Slavic Congress at Prague in 1848, and did much to popularize science in his homeland.

Pushkin, Aleksandr Sergeyevich (1799–1837): 25, 50, 66

Pypin, Aleksandr Nikolayevich (1833–1904): 41
Pypin was a well-known Russian scholar who specialized in Slavic literatures and folklore. He viewed literature as an expression of national consciousness. Among his major works are a two-volume *History of Slavic Literatures* (co-authored with V. D. Spasovich) and a four-volume *History of Russian Literature*.

Raitz, Alexander (1799–1862): 43
Raitz was a Baltic German historian of Russian law. He was the first professor of Russian jurisprudence at Dorpat University. His *Versuch über die geschichtliche Ausbildung der russischen Staats- und Rechtsverfassung* (1829) was the first attempt at a complete and systematic history of Russian law up to the Code of 1649.

Repin, Ilya Yefimovich (1844–1930): 65
Repin was an outstanding Russian historical painter. His compositions are remarkable for their dramatic force and characterization.

Rieger, František Ladislav (1818–1903): 80–81, 87–88, 136
Rieger was a major Czech political and cultural leader. He represented the more conservative element in the nationalist movement (the Old Czech party). He was a representative at the Kroměříž (Kremsier) Parliament. After its dispersal he lived in exile in France until 1851. Upon his return he married Palacký's daughter and published the first Czech encyclopedia, *Riegrův Slovník naučný* (11 vols., 1858–74). In 1861 he founded *Národní listy* (*The National Paper*), the first important Czech newspaper, and won election to the Bohemian Diet and Austrian Reichsrat. Thirty years later he lost his seat and retired from political life.

Rokycana, Jan (c. 1397–1471): 12–13
Rokycana was one of the most important Hussite theologians and leaders. He represented the conservative wing of the movement. A gifted preacher, he became minister of the Týn church in 1427 and headed the clergy of the Prague party. He was appointed rector of Prague University in 1435. That same year he was elected archbishop of the Hussite church; in this capacity he signed the peace treaty with the Council of Basel in 1436.

Rokytanský, Karel (Rokitansky, Karl) (1804–78): 114
Rokytanský was a famous pathologist. Born at Hradec Králové (Königgrätz), he studied medicine at Prague and Vienna where he became professor of pathological anatomy in 1834. He was elected president of the Vienna Academy of Sciences in 1869. His major work was *Handbuch der pathologischen Anatomie* (3 vols., 1842–46).

Rousseau, Jean-Jacques (1712–78): 25, 29, 33, 36, 61, 72, 79, 80, 82, 107

Rurik (ninth century): 36
Rurik is the traditional founder of the Russian state. He was a Varangian prince who, according to the Primary Chronicle, accepted the Slavs' invitation to rule over them.

Šafařík, Pavel Josef (1795–1861): 13–14, 18–19, 21–22, 25, 28, 31, 40–41, 42, 43–44, 47–48, 50–52, 56–57, 58, 60, 62, 66, 73, 79, 84, 95, 114, 124, 129–30, 132
Šafařík was a Slovak scholar who became one of the greatest Slavists of the nineteenth century. He studied philology, philosophy, history, natural sciences, mathematics, and astronomy at Jena (1815–17). There he became acquainted with Dobrovský's and Palacký's writings. He left Jena as an ardent Slav patriot and an enthusiastic proponent of Slavic reciprocity. Upon his return home he met Palacký; they became intimate friends and published together *Počátkové českého básnictví* (1818). In 1819 Šafařík was appointed professor and director of the Orthodox gymnasium at Novi Sad. There he studied Serbian literature and published a series of works on it including the first critical edition of Old Serbian monuments. He also published his *Geschichte der slavischen Sprache und Literatur nach allen Mundarten* (1826–27), which remained the standard work of its kind for fifty years and was the source for other such histories (e.g., that of Pypin and Spasovich). This work had a great influence on the development of Slavic studies among the Russians, Poles, and southern Slavs. In 1833 Šafařík moved to Prague. There he published another great work, *Slovanské starožitnosti* (*Slavic Antiquities*, 1837). Under very difficult conditions he produced other important works: *Památky dřevního písemnictví Jihoslovanů* (*Monuments of the South Slavs' Early Literature*, 1851), *Památky hlaholského písemnictví* (*Monuments of Glagolitic Literature*, 1853) and *Über den Ursprung und die Heimath des Glagolitismus* (1858).

Schelling, Friedrich Wilhelm Joseph (1775–1854): 25
Schelling was a German philosopher who developed a metaphysical system based on *Naturphilosophie*. A student of Kant, Fichte, and Spinoza, he was professor of philosophy at Jena from 1798 to 1803. Later Schelling held a professorship at Munich.

Schlözer, August Ludwig (1735–1809): 43
Schlözer was an eminent German historian, statistician, and publicist. He was appointed professor of Russian history by Catherine II.

Schwarzenberg, Friedrich, Prince (1809–85): 91
Schwarzenberg was an Austrian prince who became Archbishop of Prague in 1850.

Seibt, Karel Jindřich (1735–1806): 36
Seibt was a humanist and a professor at the University of Prague. He lectured on ethics, pedagogy, German stylistics, and history. Imbued with the ideas of English, French, and German philosophers (Hume, Voltaire, Montesquieu, etc.), he influenced both Dobrovský and Jungmann.

Shevyrev, Stepan Petrovich (1806–64): 56
Shevyrev was professor of literature at Moscow University, a literary critic, and a Slavophile.

Škoda, Josef (1805–81): 114
Škoda was a renowned Czech doctor and clinician. He studied philosophy at Plzeň and medicine at Vienna, where he obtained his doctorate in 1831. In 1847 he became professor of the medical clinic in Vienna and directed it until 1871. Together with Rokytanský he is generally recognized as the leading figure of the second Viennese school of medicine.

Sladkovský, Karel (1823–80): 120, 144
Sladkovský was a Czech politician. He represented the democratic-radical Young Czech party, which was opposed to the national-liberal Old Czech faction. He published articles attacking the position of Palacký and Rieger in *Večerní List* (*The Evening Paper*). Later he became a member of the editorial board of *Národní Listy*.

Smetana, Augustin (1814–51): 18, 21, 91, 106–8, 124, 132
Smetana was a Czech philosopher who was influenced by Hegel. All of his writings are based on the idea that the present and its peoples are a transition from a material past to an ideal future. Thus the central concepts are those of evolution, transformation, and progress. His works include *Die Bestimmung unseres Vaterlandes Böhmen* (1848), *Die Bedeutung des gegenwärtigen Zeitalters* (1848), and *Der Geist, sein Entstehen und sein Vergehen* (1865).

Smetana, Bedřich (1824–84): 106
Smetana was a great Czech composer and the founder of his country's national school of music. *Má vlast* (*My Country*), a cycle of six symphonic poems, and *Prodaná nevěsta* (*The Bartered Bride*), an opera, are his most important works.

Sobyestiansky, Ivan Mikhaylovich (1856–96): 60–62, 65, 70–73, 75
Sobyestiansky was a Russian jurist who began his career by lecturing on the history of Russian law at Kharkov University. He became a professor after defending his master's and doctoral theses: "Mutual Guarantee among the Slavs" (1888) and "Studies of the National Features of the Ancient Slavs" (1893). The latter is the work to which Masaryk is referring.

Spenser, Herbert (1820–1903): 73
English philosopher and sociologist.

Stanislav of Znojmo (?–1414): 4
Stanislav of Znojmo was a prominent representative of realism at Prague University. At first he was a friend of Jan Hus, but later he became an adversary. We do not have much information about his life. He obtained his master's and doctor's degrees in theology. He was appointed dean of the Faculty of Arts. From the beginning he was a very ardent adherent of Wycliffe's doctrine, and he went much farther in his acceptance of it than Hus. His final break with Hus occurred in 1412 in the famous dispute over indulgences. When King Wenceslaus banished Hus's four most intransigent opponents from Prague, Stanislav was one of these men.

Sternberg, Kaspar (1761–1838): 41
Count Sternberg was one of the founders of the Bohemian Museum in 1818. He was an eminent botanist who wrote *Abhandlung der Pflanzenkunde in Böhmen* (1817–18). His memoirs were edited by Palacký.

Štítný, Tomáš (c. 1331 to c. 1401): 4, 5
Štítný was a Czech lay writer whose works present a Christian-philosophical view of the world. His major writings are contained in a series of anthologies under the title *Knížky šestery o obecných věcech křest'anských* (*Six Booklets on General Christian Matters*) and in his *Řeči besední* (*Friendly Talks*). Štítný provided Czech literature with its first classic prose works.

Stritter, Johann Gotthilf (1740–1801): 43, 66
Stritter was a German historian who worked in the archives of the Russian college of foreign affairs and was an assistant at the Academy of Sciences. One of his works provides information about the Slavs and the history of Old Russia on the basis of Byzantine sources. He also wrote a history of Russia up to the year 1462 in German.

Štúr, Ľudevít (1815–56): 56
Štúr was a leading Slovak poet, writer, organizer, and politician. In the years 1847–49 he was one of the organizers of Slovak political and armed resistance against the Hungarians, and he participated in the activities of the Pan-Slavic Congress at Prague. His writings reflect his idealism, his Pan-Slavism, and the influence of Hegel's philosophy.

Surowiecki, Wawrzyniec (1769–1827): 53, 56, 60, 62
Surowiecki was a Polish historian and publicist. He wrote a treatise on the origins of the Slavic peoples which provoked Šafařík to write *Über die Abkunft der Slaven nach Lorenz Surowiecki* (1828).

Sušil, František (1804–68): 91
Sušil was a Moravian priest, professor, and awakener whose main works are his three collections of Moravian folk songs (1835, 1840, 1853–60) and his *Písmo svaté Nového Zákona* (*The Holy Scripture of the New Testament*). The folk song collections became a documentary source of dialectology and national music, while his "explication" of the New Testament was a work unique in all of Slavdom.

Suvorov, Aleksandr Vasilyevich (1729–1800): 27
Suvorov was a renowned Russian general whose military feats helped Catherine the Great expand and consolidate her empire.

Světlá, Karolina (1830–99) (pseudonym of Johanna Mužáková): 104
Světlá was a prolific Czech novelist. She is noted for her treatment of the woman's question and for her realistic description of Czech life.

Szymanowski, Józef (1748–1801): 35
Szymanowski was a renowned poet of the Polish classical school. He owes his reputation mainly to a verse elaboration of Montesquieu's "Temple of Gnidos."

Tablic, Bohuslav (1769–1832): 47
Tablic was an evangelical minister and Czechoslovak writer. As a poet he belonged to Puchmajer's school. He published his verse under the title *Poezye* (4 vols., 1806–12). His extensive introductory essays to these volumes as well as his anthology of Slovak poetry, *Slovenské veršovce* (*Slovak Poets*, 2 vols., 1805–9) comprised his main contribution to Czechoslovak literary history.

Tatishchev, Vasily Nikitich (1686–1750): 43
Tatishchev was a well-known Russian historian. His major work entitled *Russian History* (5 vols.) was published posthumously (1768–1848). It is more a critical comparison of the chronicles than a history. The author's comments reflect knowledge of the writings of Hobbes, Bayle, and Locke.

Tolstoy, Lev Nikolayevich (1828–1910): 66, 126

Tomek, Václav Vladivoj (1818–1905): 17, 91
Tomek is the most famous Czech historian aside from Palacký. Among his numerous works are *Děje země české* (*History of the Czech Land*, 1843), *Děje university Pražské* (*History of Prague University*, 1848), *Dějepis města Prahy* (*History of Prague*, 12 vols., 1855–1901), *Geschichte Böhmens in übersichtlicher Darstellung* (1864), and *Jan Žižka* (1879).

Turgenev, Ivan Sergeyevich (1818–83): 66

Tyl, Josef Kajetán (1808–56): 79, 99
Tyl was a writer, journalist, producer, and theater director. He edited the journal *Květy* (*Flowers*); wrote, translated, and produced plays; directed theaters; and became the most popular short-story writer of his time. Tyl was primarily a publicist who supported patriotic, educational, and humanitarian causes.

Vocel, Jan Erazim (1803–71): 50
Vocel was a Czech poet, awakener, archaeologist, and cultural historian. Until 1834 his works appeared in German; then he became a Czech poet and a leading spokesman of Czech national thought. In 1838 he published a cycle of poems called *Přemyslovci* (*The Premyslids*) that were well received. Two other cycles, *Meč a kalich* (*The Sword and the Chalice*, 1843) and *Labyrint slávy* (*The Labyrinth of Glory*, 1846), completed this historical trilogy. In 1850 Vocel became professor extraordinary of Czech archaeology and history of art at the University of Prague. He published numerous articles and the important *Pravěk země české* (*The Primeval Age of the Czech Land*, 2 vols., 1866–68).

Voigt, Mikuláš (1733–87): 21, 34
Voigt was a Czech historian and awakener. A remarkably learned man, he was one of the most outstanding precursors of Dobrovský.

Voltaire (François Marie Arouet) (1694–1778): 25, 47, 89, 102, 107, 116

Voss, Johann Heinrich (1751–1826): 50
Voss was a poet whose translations of Homer—*The Odyssey* (1781) and *The Iliad* (1793)—secured him a permanent place in German literature.

Vydra, Stanislav (1741–1801): 21, 47
Vydra was a Czech awakener and mathematician. A Jesuit, he wrote a German life of Bohuslav Balbín (1788) and a Latin history of mathematics in Bohemia and Moravia (1778).

Wieland, Christoph Martin (1733–1813): 47, 89, 102
Wieland was an influential German poet and prose writer. He wrote

the first educational novel (*Geschichte des Agathon*, 1766–67) and translated most of Shakespeare (twenty-two plays, 1762–66).

Wycliffe, John (1320?–84), English reformer: 5, 6, 70

Yazykov, Nikolay Mikhaylovich (1803–46): 50
Yazykov was one of the leading Russian poets of the 1820s. He was on good terms with the nationalist and Slavophile circles in Moscow.

Zahradník, Vincenc (1790–1836): 21
Zahradník was a Czech priest and writer. He was appointed professor of pastoral theology at Litoměřice in 1820, but he was soon removed from this position for his adherence to Bolzano's ideas. Subsequently he was sent to a remote village. In addition to his philosophical writings he published a collection of fables (1832).

Zdziechowski, Marjan (1861–1938): 101
Zdziechowski was a Polish literary and cultural historian, publicist and professor of Slavic philology at the University of Cracow. He wrote a study on Mácha and Czech Byronism.

Zelený, Václav (1825–75): 44, 55
Zelený was a Czech literary historian and politician. He became professor of history and geography at the Academic Gymnasium in Prague in 1850. As a politician he was close to Palacký and Rieger. He wrote a life of Jungmann (*Život Josefa Jungmanna*) in 1873.

Zhukovsky, Vasily Andreyevich (1783–1852): 50
Zhukovsky was the first important Russian poet of the nineteenth century, a remarkable translator (e.g., Homer's *Odyssey*) and a leading figure in the literary world of his time.

Ziegler, Josef Liboslav (1782–1846): 91
Ziegler was a Czech writer and awakener.

Žižka, Jan (c. 1376–1424): 4, 6, 8–9, 11, 13, 47, 65
Žižka was a great Czech warrior and national hero. He led the Hussites against King Sigismund and the Catholic forces in a series of successful military campaigns.